STAY CENTERED
PSYCHIC
WARRIOR

A Psychic Medium's Trip Through the Darkness and Light

of the Physical and Spirit Worlds,

and Other Paranormal Phenomena

KEVIN HUNTER

WARRIOR
OF LIGHT
PRESS

Warrior of Light Press
www.kevin-hunter.com

First Edition: April 2019
Printed in the United States of America

All rights reserved. Copyright © 2019
ISBN-13: 978-0578481692

3. Mind and Body. 2. Spirituality. 1. Title

Contents

Preface

Out of the dozens of books I've written and published to date, this one in particular has been a longtime in the making. The idea came to me years prior to its release, but I had continued to shelve it. This one hits close to home because it deals with the personal torment and struggle I've had in the trenches of the physical world intertwined with the saving grace of the spirit worlds. Sometimes the two intersect so severely that it can create a triple header tsunami within me. Navigating through this Earthly life has been a challenging one to stay afloat, but my soul knew this was how it would be.

In childhood, my professional interest was to one day write books. It wasn't to be a psychic or start a spiritual practice. Because of the Divine psychic information I've had within me since childhood, the side effect was being thrust into the role of a metaphysical, philosophical, parapsychologist teacher, but I just wanted to be a creative artist that wrote books. I am blessed that the childhood dream had been made a reality.

I grew up in a volatile and toxic home full of massive ongoing traumatic child abuse that caused my soul to permanently break apart while creating irreversible psychological mental damage. This led to the additional side effects of being plagued by an array of anxiety disorders and addictions. On the opposite end, I had this infinite profound psychic foresight since childhood that has been both a gift and a curse. The gift being that it helped me adequately assess situations, hone in on answers, endure numerous soul transformations, while seizing practical opportunities in life with grand confidence. The curse being due to how potently overpowering the psychic input can be while aggravated by the human mental complexities placed on an exceptionally sensitive soul. Absorbing every incoming psychic nuance and vibration from both the physical and spirit worlds can be a challenging one, but through the power of the Light, I have been sanctioned to know that my Divine role as a warrior soul means you are trained to withstand any storm.

In *Stay Centered Psychic Warrior*, I talk about what it's like battling between mental health issues along with the deeply potent psychic input that continuously falls into my soul's consciousness throughout each day. I discuss the many examples of my encounters with spirit, as well as the seeing and hearing of the dead, although I use the word *dead* with irony, since they're not technically dead. In this, I also dive deep into something I've rarely found discussed, and that is the power of the darkness that exists in both the physical and spirit worlds. There will also be some fun stuff on my numerous personal psychic and mediumship scenarios. There will be some glimpses and reveals of the Other Side, and some distinctive traits that indicate how much more powerful my soul is compared to me in this human body on Earth. My soul is in there somewhere the same way your soul is beating around deep in the core of your physical being as well too. We'll touch deeply on the soul, as well as how to recognize your own psychic gifts, and much more.

Some of what is discussed in this will include

messages, guidance, visions, and wisdom from my Spirit team intertwined with the rest of the content. What they tell me or show me surrounding certain things isn't saying this is the way it is. Like any translator, I'm just relaying what I'm being shown, enlightened about, or informed on. If your soul feels intensely opposed to what they're relaying, then trust your instincts. If I use the word God, I am not referring to the God that some associate with Hell and Damnation. Feel free to substitute the word with one you're more comfortable with like Universe, Spirit, Creator, the Light, and so on. The same goes for the instances where I refer to God as He. Use the pronoun you're most comfortable with. All of my work is non-denominational, which means my Spirit team and I act the way Heaven does which is with welcome arms no matter your race, gender, sexual orientation, political affiliation or any other label your human experience chooses to identify with this lifetime.

I'm aware I'm unique and different, which means I may not be everyone's cup of tea, so if this isn't for you then donate it, give it to someone you know that will like the content, or just randomly toss it through the window of a passing vehicle. I can be bluntly direct without apology when I communicate and I don't shy away from the Darkness. My interest in life is doing what God called me here to do and not for human validation. The work is what I stay focused and centered on. If anything I hope you enjoy this. Perhaps it may inspire and empower you to break through the rubble of the Earthly plane and stand strong and centered under the powerful Light that shines through any crushing Darkness.

With love,
Kevin Hunter

Kevin Hunter

STAY CENTERED
PSYCHIC WARRIOR

CHAPTER ONE

The Brush With Spirit

The first run-ins with Spirit I recall were around four years old, so it's been going on for as long as I can remember. Your memories of childhood are filed away even though you may not remember much the older and further away from that age you get. Some research studies have cited age seven to be the earliest age that people can remember things. They never talked to me about it, because I can recall the first cases of my psychic abilities already in full force by the time I was four. I wish I could say that it's an awesome feeling, but not always.

Seeing a Spirit in a coat with long hair move out of my bedroom gave me the biggest fright that accelerated my breath and heart rate, because I knew it wasn't human or my imagination. There was no doubt about what it was to me at that age. I was wide awake, clear minded, conscious, and not on anything. I couldn't tell if it was a male or female as it appeared to be androgynous, neither male or female. I quickly grew to recognizing the differences between them over the years that followed. For instance, artwork or statues show Angels and Archangels as a man or a woman, when in truth they are androgynous having no genital anatomy. God has them show up as human to resemble something familiar to people. Like all Spirits, they can morph into however they choose to appear for someone from that androgynous palette. That was one of the first clearest human recollections I have of Spirit from the beginnings of this particular Earth life. As I grew older and my suppressed memories of Spirit diminished, I've had never ending memories of those on the Other Side flush up over the course of my life.

From the age of four, the Spirit run-ins increased dramatically. It was like the story of the Christmas Carol in a sense where a different spirit being was visiting me every few days. I quickly realized that they come in peace...most of them anyway. My child mind relaxed into that comfort and to this day has yet to falter. The first number of times I was fearful as most any child would be of anything they thought to be seen as new. I'm known as extremely guarded today, but that guardedness was there as a child too, so naturally the on guardedness continued with Spirit in the beginning.

I was becoming fully aware of the spirit beings around me during toddler years and the early human developmental phase. This is the same way you become aware of who your parents are at a young age. Initially, I remember climbing into the closet and shutting the doors to peer through the cracks waiting for the spirits to leave. It was the only time I was fearful of them the way certain pets you bring home are fearful, then once they're comfortable with you they come out and play. That's how I am with new people in general. Although I don't physically hide, but I do step back guarded, distant, and almost hostile, as I'm silently psychically reading them to make sure the person is okay to allow in or not. If they're not, then I can't get out of there and away from them fast enough. With Spirit, I realized they came in peace and that they were a part of me.

The back to back psychic phenomenon's taking place in early childhood were coming in on a grand scale that would never lighten up. Another incident that comes to mind was around the same age of four. I walked into my bedroom one morning seeing the bright sunshine streaming through the window. Standing under the doorframe was a horrifying sight that caused my body to grow heavier. My bed was covered in disgusting insects as I looked on in disbelief. I then looked over at the toy chest near the bed to see all of these creepy-crawly things swarming all over my toys. Fearlessly moving towards the toy chest I frantically began throwing my toys out of the box to try and get rid of them.

My mother informed me she remembered that day. She heard me in the room and came rushing in to see what was the matter. I pointed and said, "Bugs."

Moving towards the toy box with concern looking around she said, "There isn't anything there. It's just your imagination."

You know like adults say when a child says they're seeing something they can't see. Sometimes it might be their imagination, but you also have to keep an open mind that it may not be their imagination. Children especially have some of the strongest psychic sense channels. The reason is they're not jaded and blocked the way adults become as they grow older due to life's challenges, disappointments, distractions, and Earthly physical pleasures that all contribute to fogging up ones psychic vision. Most of those children with the strong psychic channels will witness them dim over time due to the same life challenges and blocks, unless their parents support and develop these gifts.

Due to the ever growing popularity of spiritual interests, we're seeing a larger open mindedness to all things related to spirituality. We've come a long way from the days when people were killed for exhibiting psychic related behavior. Humankind was superstitious and fearful that they would kill anyone for displaying any kind of conduct that was different than anyone else, let alone if they appeared to be psychic in some way.

The spirit episodes I began noticing as a child never diminished the way they might for other jaded adults. The psychic phenomena grew to be repetitive that it caused panic and concern from my Mother. She initially thought there might be some kind of underlying serious medical issue going on. Seeing her child knocking things away that no one else could see would be cause for concern beyond it being part of the imagination. Everything checked out medically by the open minded Doctor who eventually said, "Consider the fact that you have a gifted child on your hands."

Medically everything checked out fine, except for something interesting. One of them being that they found partial physical hearing loss and partial sight on the same side of my body. The reason that's noteworthy is that half of my Earthly physical senses are fainter than the other half. The physical half part of me that is fainter, the volume of spirit is louder on that side through hearing (clairaudience), knowing (claircognizance), and vision (clairvoyance). It's an interesting psychic phenomena to make note of. The Clairsentience is all over my spiritual and physical body.

While human beings are flawed and will inevitably mess up, spirits Love is constant and unwavering. When I connect with God and Spirit, they pull me up into a wave of love that is better than anything I've ever experienced and I've experienced plenty! I couldn't write thousands of pages of text without them, especially with my restless ADD. The one area my ADD is not present is when I'm writing.

If one is too absorbed on the surface of things to comprehend what's going on beyond the physical, then it is unlikely they are in touch with the psychic touch. The touch is being in tune to spirit and the vibrations from beyond. It doesn't mean they are incapable of that kind of deep spirit connection, because they do have the power deep down within them to access it. Every single soul has that same power, whether they know it or not, and regardless of their human belief limitations. I am psychic and so are you! It would be nice if everyone was aware of it because then Earth would be as close to Heaven as feasibly possible. There would be never-ending joy, peace, and love for every soul. Everyone would be operating from a higher vibration and moving mountains in the process. We see this kind of amazing uplifting joy in others when they're in a high vibrational state. Because this is not the current reality where everyone is functioning in that space, this makes Earthly life more challenging than it should be. It is either ourselves or other people that create the majority of problems that happen in the physical world. Once in awhile Mother Earth creates catastrophes, since this rock we temporarily inhabit has a life force of its own.

If you have major anxiety, then you may be more psychic than you believe. The anxiety comes from the erratic energies within and around you. There is no break from absorbing the psychic energies, because it never stops. It takes enormous energy out of me every second. I have to navigate my life in an incredibly strict way to ensure complete protection, and sometimes that's not even enough for it. The more in tune and psychic you are, the higher your anxiety likely is.

The psychic system is a fragile instrument that is overloaded with information and stimuli on every breath, which is not exciting. To some it's weird, to some it's cool, but it's neither of those things to me. It's often challenging, draining, and confusing. You cannot wake up one day and ask to unsubscribe from your purpose or quit God's service. There is no out!

Super sensitive's will try to drown and control their anxiety and emotions with the use of drugs, pills, cigarettes, food, alcohol, or any other toxic addiction, which is what I did. You're basically covering a cut with a band aid. There is no way to permanently stop it even if you are using toxins to block the spirit energy from entering. It's part of our make-up and it is what it is. You learn to live with it and use it to your advantage when possible.

As I progressed into adulthood, I began to channel it through positive endeavors and choices. Part of that is to be of service through my life purpose work and in helping someone else through Earthly challenges as best I can. That's the #1 area I feel a sense of relief because the gifts are being utilized the way it's supposed to be, but that doesn't make it any easier. It just distracts me enough to focus on where it's doing its best work.

CHAPTER TWO

I See and Hear Dead People

Spirit beings appear physically whole the first number of seconds from my peripheral vision. As I become aware of their presence they dissolve into a translucent figure that tells me they are not a human being on the physical Earth plane. They are physical back home on the Other Side, but through the separation veil between the Earth plane and Heaven and the higher realms, they come through translucent. They may at first glance appear physical to me through Clairvoyance, but as that fades and I see them through the veil they appear translucent. This is due to the heavy etheric substances between both planes. It's like seeing someone under water that it's almost dream like.

One afternoon a friend and I were taking a road trip through a nature part of California, which I love to do. I was driving down one of the roads and I did a double take when this woman popped up out of nowhere in front of me on the road. I went into flight mode and swerved off the road skidding my tires in a panic to avoid hitting her. Due to being about fifteen seconds away from ramming into her, this prompted me to react in a panic with a string of expletives. "What the....is she walking in the middle of the street for!?"

My perplexed friend looked around out his window coming down from his panic that I induced.

"There's nobody there." He said confused.

Hands gripped to the steering wheel as I looked out the front window and then the driver's side window.

"She was just there." I said equally puzzled.

Scanning the area again I pulled back noticing her re-appear on the side of the road moving towards the forest of trees where she dissolved into an opaque figure, and then faded away. My rapid breath slowed down into a calmness, "Never mind. She wasn't a human being."

Mostly I brush it off ignoring it, but there are times I look like I'm crazy talking to the air or driving off the road as described. Some of my connections and encounters are similar that it leads me to believe someone has a staring problem. As I grow aggravated by being watched, I look again and realize it's an angel or spirit being. It's uncomfortable having people stand too close to me especially someone I don't know. A former colleague and now friend commented that he noticed this with me. He pointed out, "When people take a step towards you, I noticed you always take a step away."

Part of this is due to the energies I'm absorbing off them, which can be too much to take on my psychic system. When I realize someone is staring at me I am sometimes vocal about it, "What are you looking at?"

I turn my head realizing it's not human and then I feel only slightly ridiculous.

My Mother had also informed me that I've always been like that and that it's nothing new. She said, "When you were little and we went out, it would bother you when people were looking at you. You would say, "What are they looking at?"

This is also part of being hyper-vigilante. The fact that my soul is a Warrior soul in general, it would make sense that the hyper alertness was present as a child as well too. Knights, Hunters, Soldiers, Kings, and Warriors all have that similar observant nature as they're trained to be on guard. Unfortunately, this also carries over to harmless episodes where someone comes in peace too.

I SEE DEAD PEOPLE. That line has always sounded silly because there is no real death. People are not technically dead. They are dead in the sense that the body is lifeless and no longer functioning. It is clear there is no life or life force in the body anymore. The spirit soul that inhabited that body has been freed from that confinement. It has been freed into another sphere of consciousness, another plane of existence, and parallel universe alongside this one.

The dead are amongst us on Earth, but they're not dead in the way one might believe them to be dead. They're no longer weighed down and strangled by this ego dominated false reality that force feeds a fictional superficial shallow view of human life. The real death and Hell is living on a planet that lacks in love with minimal to no awareness or mind blowing perception. This isn't saying that no one is like that, because there are a great many souls on the planet that are filled with love, operate from love, and give love. They also have enormous awareness and mind blowing foresight. The majority on the planet however do not reside in that space. Because if they did, then that would be evident in the physical world's culture and it's not. The dominate rule on Earth is the darkness of ego. This is why one quarter of the planet is here with a purpose to counter that with their Light. You are a way shower in this manner even if it changes one person that ends up changing another and so forth. This is how a mighty positive movement of change happens Universally.

We have been moving into a period where more souls are incarnating with this grand awareness of love. There has been a growing movement of people seeking ways to find fulfillment and happiness. Some call this the New Age, but it's not New Age it's the soul's reality. If the New Age is about displaying love, then feel free to drink a healthy helping of it. The New Age teaches about self love and that you are your own authority. To one extent this is true, but there is a higher authority that some call God, the Universe, Spirit, or however you choose to label it. Many will fidget or grow uncomfortable when the word God is said. This is due to the excessive negative way it's been used in horrific ways by Nazi-like fanatical religious groups. They will hide behind the God or Jesus Christ name to harm, hate, and harass other people claiming they're doing it out of love. Regardless of what label you choose to use, God is the ultimate authority to partner with in order to find that eternal soul happiness. Human beings cannot do everything alone and why would you want to when you have willing guardians available to help, protect, and guide you to become a stronger person and a more evolved soul in the process.

I've been seeing the dead moving about since I first

recalled consciousness. Laying up at night as a five year old battling insomnia that still never ceases, I'd sit up in bed and watch spirit figures entering and exiting my room, seeing them across the playground at school, appearing next to me on a chair. Moving about in the physical world I'm not immediately aware that the person standing beside me is technically in another plane. This is one of the reasons I sometimes appear jumpy. It's not the kind of jumpiness connected to fear, but jumpiness where I'm instantly startled to find someone standing next to me staring. It's like someone saying, "Boo!"

You would jolt for a startled beat with a quick gasp inhale. It doesn't matter that I've experienced this more times than can be counted or recorded. It is still not something you ever get used to. The startle is for a fleeting second when you discover someone or a spirit is standing there, then it's brushed off as I continue on with life.

As a younger child around the ages of four to six, I was still too young to understand who they were when I was hiding from them. My Mother would be looking for me and find me hiding in the closet peering through the cracks to see if they've left. I'd explain that there is someone else in the house.

At first she would panic, "What? Where?"

She'd look around. "There's no one here. It's just your imagination."

Eventually, I became more comfortable with seeing them after realizing most of them were not a threat. Once that happened my etheric senses began to shift where their voices grew louder and Clairaudience became the dominate way they've communicated with me. When you have Clairaudience, then the way that

Spirit communicates with you is through the etheric hearing psychic sense channel. To me it sounds like someone is standing next to me talking to me. Sometimes they will shout if I'm not listening or if I'm talking to someone else and it's important. Other times I can be having conversations with someone about things and I hear a Spirit team council member chiming in, which prompts me to say what they're saying out loud. The person I'm talking to will confirm it, "Yeah, that's right actually. Wait, how did you know that?"

By the time I was seven and eight years old, I was fully aware of the people around me that were not human. Today I know them to be my council or Spirit team, but as a child they had no name or label since I automatically just knew who they were via telepathy and knowingness, which is part of having Claircognizance. I'd be playing outside with friends in childhood while occasionally hearing the voices of spirit communicating with me. I was coming to terms with them while responding out loud. I had to learn to tone that part down, so as not to appear as a crazy person. Even though there are still times I'm responding out loud not thinking about it. You're reacting and responding the way you might if anyone approached you and was talking to you. You would respond out loud. I learned to do my best to keep my responses to them internally while out and about with strangers around, since Spirit are telepathic and able to hear your thoughts through that avenue anyway. Being out with friends I don't need to hide that as they know me and know what to expect.

As I became fully accustomed and acclimated with them by the time I was seven and eight years old, I'd sometimes venture off alone outside on my bike or through a walk in nature or somewhere quiet. This helped me to have private conversations with them while in a nature setting. Those were the locations I discovered where the psychic information would come through stronger. This is also one of the reasons I've preached to get out into nature. It's more powerful than any Church without the confines of human made concrete. This isn't saying don't go to Church if you enjoy that. I knew early on they were with me wherever I was. I felt completely safe with them and that safety has never wavered since. They were there all throughout the childhood abuse I endured at home and through my rebellious toxic addiction years in my late teens and early twenties. They were always there around me and have never left. I've received an enormously valuable life class on the soul and psychic phenomena through them.

Growing up being able to connect with them I began to realize that no one seemed to observe the same traits of having any measurable psychic foresight, even though they have the abilities within them. As a result, I started to feel alone and separate from others for a period of time. This isn't to be confused with loneliness. I just felt set apart and solo the way a warrior soul would be. Those that recalled me in childhood had pointed out that as a child I seemed to march around independently head up eyes forward completely serious and determined. I stepped into those shoes naturally accepting that I was different than the human societal norms, which has never bothered me and to this day has yet to change.

Throughout my teenage years I became the go to person for counseling by my peers. Every clique you can imagine in High School would be coming to talk to me alone about what they were going through. This was from the cliché titles of the geek, the jock, the techie, the cheerleader, the drama student, and onwards. I became the kid counselor that prompted them to say the same things repeatedly with ecstatic relief, "God you always know just what to say that fixes an issue! It's like you're this old soul that's a hundred years old, but you're this sixteen year old in High School. It's really cool."

These counselor like qualities only expanded as I moved into adulthood. There was a former boss I worked with during the film business days who pointed out that I struck him as someone that was friends with everyone in High School like the jock, the bookworm, the popular guy, the not so popular guy, the cheerleader, the valedictorian, etc. I explained he was right and while I had my own super close trusted circle of friends, I was also friends with others beyond that. I have no judgment or interest in popularity, so I'm not going to be friends with someone because they are part of a label or a group. I will be friends with them based on the depths of their soul and human character. In each of those cliques there are some of those treasured gems that reveal elements of the depths existing in their soul. They suppressed it while in those groups, but not while with me. People feel as if they can be as unique as they like in my presence the same way they can with Spirit.

As for the psychic stuff, there was still a sense of feeling apart from everyone else, which can feel isolating at times. It wasn't until the Internet started up and then social media when other similar people came forward through technology. It's given me some measure of reality that there are others with stronger gifts or that have spiritual related interests, but it hasn't ever completely diminished the separate feeling that still exists. I learned that is also the mark of a warrior who travels independently, solo, strong with leadership qualities that transcend what society is doing. Besides in general I rub people either the right way or the wrong way, but looking for Universal acceptance has never been on my radar of interest. The Universal acceptance I look for and always receive comes from Heaven, so that's more than enough for me. Universal acceptance doesn't exist in the human reality so chasing popularity is a wasteful cause. You're not taking any of those social media followers, likes, reviews, or awards with you when you die.

Sometimes my Spirit team guides speak in turns and other times in unison. Their voices have always been across the board in sounding male, female, and sometimes genderless and unknown. Some of them are compassionate and sensitive, but there are also the task master authoritative dominating ones too. Hearing those strong ones it was easy to detect that they were the warrior souls. Hearing the hyper intelligent ones are the teacher souls, both of which are also known as part of the Wise One soul breed. The compassionate sensitive ones were of the angelic variety.

They all mostly tend to stand to my left on the side slightly behind me. They've mostly always communicated with me through my left ear, through the left eye in my peripheral vision, and the left side of my consciousness. As mentioned, my human senses on the left side of my face and body are dimmer than the right, such as my left hearing is deafer than the right, and my left eye vision has always been fainter than the right. It's also challenging for me to sleep on the left side of my body. The left side of me is dimmer physically, but spiritually the volume of spirit is turned way up more than the right side. It's a phenomenon I've been aware of, but never questioned since the answer is clear. Another interesting irony is when I've received that rare tension headache it seems to show up on the left side of my head before the top crown and on down to the ear area.

Those that are born deaf or partially deaf tend to have a stronger clairaudience channel. They also tend to have other senses that are double what others might have. This is regardless of whether they believe it or not. They can develop it easier even if they're unaware of the gifts. You also don't have to work hard to turn off the physical world noises as those sounds are already turned off. This would be the same for someone physically blind, then they would likely have a stronger spiritual sight, which is called Clairvoyance. This is because they don't have the distraction of physical sight.

Communicating with my Spirit team was never unusual to me. I always assumed everyone had the same deal, and while they do, a great majority of people are unaware of it. As a child I never thought about where they were coming from. I wasn't thinking they were spirit beings or they were in Heaven, since there was no label that I attributed to them. What I knew for sure was that they were definitely not human like human beings, even though they may appear like that, but I knew they were not living an Earthly life. I knew they were close enough that it seemed as if they were right next to me. By the time I was about nine or ten years old, I can remember envisioning them almost like officials or judges on the Other Side sitting in chairs behind a long white table. Wherever I went they were there, and wherever I go they are with me. There was no running from them, but not like I wanted to. I've always thought of them as both family members and best friends that know more about me than any human being on the planet. They have forever been able to hear my thoughts and I hear their voices in response to some of my thoughts. I knew they were real because many of the things they'd share with me or tell me would end up later coming true.

Hearing crazy voices will not be telling you something that ends up being true.

While most of the time they are on my left, once in a rare moon they may show up on the right, but more often than not they are on the left. The clear hearing Clairaudience is strongest in my etheric left ear where the physical ear hearing is dim. Spirit is louder in that deafer ear. The left side of my physical body is a stronger psychic tool than the right. None of this means that Spirit is always on the left side for every single person. Everyone is given the gifts of psychic clair senses to be able to connect and communicate with God and Spirit through those psychic senses. It is up to every individual on the planet to do the work to discover which of their senses are the strongest. This is the same way that someone's Aunt has strong Clairvoyance, but their best friend has strong Claircognizance. It's also the same way that someone who conducts readings may use the Tarot, while another may use angel cards, someone else an angel board, while another uses no divination tool except their own body. Over the course of someone's life, they gradually discover where their own strongest gifts reside.

Hearing others make fun of psychics only gets an internal eye roll, because it's a redundant and untrue statement considering that they also have psychic gifts within them. If they raised their vibration above the limited view of judgment, then they would start to pick up on it for themselves too. Some people have to work much harder to bring that out. You cannot be a lazy child of God never trying to evolve your soul. Yeah, that never goes over well in the end.

I don't typically use any tools to communicate with God except my own psychic clair senses. There may be times that I feel blocked from certain messages or I want to confirm an important message. This is where a Divination tool like cards can help, but 99% of the time I use my own spirit soul vessel as the Divination tool. The reason is not because I think it's better, but because it was just how Spirit personally trained me early on.

When I was a child and having these spiritual psychic connections, pulling cards or using a tool never crossed my mind. I had never heard of that at age five. They were coming through me automatically on their own and I picked up on it naturally through my soul. It's the dominate way I receive Divine psychic related information. There were no lessons, classes, videos, or seminars I took, because to my knowledge they didn't exist when I was growing up the way they do now. When I want to receive an answer to something that I'm struggling with, then I'll finally stop running around restlessly. I will say to my team, "Okay, let's talk for a minute guys. I'm going to sit down and just have a conversation with you because I need to get some answers on this. If we can all gather around for a few minutes."

I'll then ask my questions one by one. I ask the question, then the answer will either come in immediately before I finished the sentence, or a number of seconds afterwards. I quickly write it down on the pad next to me and say thank you, and then ask the next question and so forth.

Close friends have recounted me making statements to them that would later come true, so they never doubted either. When each of them were first getting to know me, they would say things like, "There's no way you could possibly know that. That's impossible."

This would continue a handful of times until they pointed out the consistency of the accuracies. They eventually became used to it and know it's just the way it is. That was another way I became a believer in what was beyond Earth, because this wasn't anything that was taught to me. I learned from Spirit on my own. There were no labels for them at the time. I did not use a label on them until much later in life, but only in cases when I needed to explain to others what they are otherwise no labels are ever used. My guides are compassionate, but extremely firm and strong. They would have to be in order to deal with my personality, which is no easy feat for anyone.

In the Clint Eastwood film, *Hereafter*, the Matt Damon character plays a psychic medium that sees his gifts of communicating with Spirit as a curse more than a gift. I found this portrayal of someone with psychic medium gifts to be more accurate for me than some of the other films that show mediums that rather enjoy communicating with the dead for others. Other enjoyable fun Hollywood films that had fully fleshed out three dimensional Psychic medium characters were Cate Blanchett in *The Gift* and Vera Farmiga in *The Conjuring*. I enjoyed those for being closer to accurate than some of the other films that portray medium's as a side gag character where the psychic medium is some crazy person with a Turban chasing people down the street to warn them of some pending doom. We saw Hollywood do this with gay characters too where they would make them the hyper flamboyant stereotypical characters as a side gag, instead of fully three dimensional characters showing all sides of someone who could be gay like a lawyer, surfer, football player, doctor, etc. This is the same with the mediumship characters, which I'd love to see more of like *Hereafter*, *The Gift*, and *The Conjuring*.

Sensing and picking up on every nuance and vibration in this world and beyond causes me more instability than stability. Not that all medium's feel this way. Due to my line of work, I have many friends in the spiritual fields as you could likely guess, and some of them love the mediumship and psychic work. They get a rushed high out of it, but they are also living in some kind of seclusion or setting that is away from people. They are just as disciplined as I am about how I navigate this planet with tempestuous human beings. That needs to be said because most of the chaos that happens to people is from other people. It's not happening with the trees, animals, or plants. It's people that are causing that friction, not all of them, which I have to say to ensure you don't assume I'm stereotyping. My Spirit team tends to speak in generalizations.

My faith and leaning on God is the stability I enjoy, but the rest of it is volatility. There's nothing fun about not being able to go to certain places because you know the energy tampering will be too rough on my psychic system. There's nothing exciting about being fearful of going outside knowing you'll run into hostile dark energies in other people. There's nothing fun about picking up on dread that exists in other souls. There's nothing fun about using my friends as shields when we go to crowded places. Having this kind of in-tune radar requires you to be exceptionally disciplined about how you navigate each day in your life. You have to make adjustments that work and discard ones that don't work.

I'm going to dive a bit deeper in the coming chapters to reveal more experiences with some of it going into darker places. Are you ready? Bring your light shield and let's keep going...

CHAPTER THREE

The Power Of the Dangerous Darkness

Part of being a psychic clear sense feeling Clairsentient is that I can go to bed happy, but then wake up buried and suffocating in anxiety and dread. This consists of sensing a darkness coming towards me, which indicates there is something unpleasant about to happen. It can be pertaining to me or someone else I know or don't know. There is no way to stop the dread, because it's a psychic premonition that doesn't always have anything to do with me or with anything I'm doing. The psychic hit comes in like an avalanche of rocks tumbling down a mountain holding dark energy.

It will also sometimes start off as a Clairvoyant dream that starts off serene, but grows darker in its symbolism as it continues on. Typically, within the next one to three days I'll find out what the psychic sense was forewarning. The problem with a Clairvoyant dream is it comes through in symbolism and the Clairsentience hits will come through the senses. It's not always being direct and exact as to what it is. The most direct way is when it comes through Clairaudience. All I know is it's something unwanted connected to me or someone I know or will run into. Nine times out of ten it will happen within a day, but sometimes it could be within a few days after that. When that's the case, then the dread continues throughout that time until it happens.

Once in awhile I will encounter a human being filled with enormous Light that brings with it this incredible uplift when they walk past me. There is a major difference felt between someone surrounded by that Light and someone surrounded by Darkness. When someone infected by the Darkness gets too close to me, then that will affect both my spiritual body and physical body since they're both connected to one another. Some of that Darkness touches me through the act of cutting into my soul's auric field. This feels like a thousand miniature razor sharp like teeth slicing across my skin repeatedly in places all around me.

Take a moment to step into that description and imagine for a second how that might feel if it were physically happening to you. It is as if someone is literally cutting you all over your body. You're experiencing the pain associated with each of those cuts on your physical body, along with the blood that seeps out of that cut, which are of differing lengths depending on how much Darkness is present. This is the case even though it's not cutting my physical body, but it feels like this is what's happening. It can range from feeling like a paper cut on up to knife wounds. This can sometimes continue on for hours throughout the day like a torture session. I'd end up walking around feeling immense pain because it doesn't go away by quickly moving physically far from the infected person. It's like catching a cold from someone where some of it has transferred, latched on, and infected me as well. It's physically impossible for me to be around it for any length of time for that reason because your physical body is also weakening in the process. Those who have a higher degree of Clairsentience feel this as well too.

There have been times I've attempted to stay in the vicinity as it's happening, but that never worked as the cuts grow deeper to the point it starts to feel like a thousand knives plunging into me. This is similar to how it would feel if you drowned in that icy cold water that the victims on the Titanic ship experienced in 1912 when it struck an iceberg in the middle of a cold night.

If this happens and there is no visible physical being around me, then at some point I will soon see all of the challenging things happening to myself or to someone around me that becomes the explain away to the dark foreboding psychic hits I received in my Clairsentient psychic sense. This is an entirely separate way that psychic communication would come in that has nothing to do with walking past an infected person. The other way is through anxiety that rises or it feels as if I'm being strangled.

The Darkness is that powerful that it can cut through an impermeable Light shield on Earth. This is another reason I can be difficult about who I'm around and where I go. It is for my soul's protection and not to ruin someone's party.

Not only can these cuts slice into me just by walking past someone contaminated by the Darkness, but other times the cuts begin to form if my own vibration has dropped or a darker entity being is trying to get close. This weakens my Light allowing the Darkness to make its move. I'm susceptible to it as anyone else, but I'm aware of when it's happening through psychically seeing, feeling, hearing, and knowing it. This is also another reason my Spirit team helps me write about this stuff, which is to help others be more conscious and aware in their own lives.

If I walk past someone carrying dark energy around them, then some of that dark energy can act like an alien-like suction cup and attach itself to my light, which causes me pain and drops my vibration in the process. It can sometimes be annoying when someone has walked too close in passing when they have this entire large space to walk. When someone is that oblivious and not psychically in tune, then they are naïve to that being a problem or that people require personal space for a reason. I'm shown that this person is not in tune to anything beyond their physical existence. This is confirmed when I pick up on the Darkness that has latched itself onto my Light because someone that had it around them walked too close. It's not like they would know that anyway. Afterwards, I'll conduct a clearing session to get the toxic gunk removed off me. It's like you're out and about and step on a nail. You have to stop and tend to it, but even after tending to it there is still some residual pain. This is another reason I'm strict and disciplined about where I go when I head outside. I'm not this way for snobbish reasons. I'm this way to protect my light from oblivious harsh souls. My survival and self-protection comes first and is beyond what someone can understand unless they have a stronger psychic touch as well too. I've conversed with many medium and psychic friends that have a stronger psychic touch, which makes it challenging for them to navigate as well. One of them said, "I hate it when someone is standing too close to me in a grocery line."

Because she's absorbing their energies and turning into a dirty dish sponge. I've had some psychically Clairsentient sensitive readers tell me over the years that they will sometimes wait until their neighbors chatter outside has gone away indicating they've left. This is to avoid having to converse with them, which of course makes me giggle. I understand that it has nothing to do with them being conceited or anti-social, but that it takes quite a bit of energy out of someone who has a stronger psychic sixth sense to be around that. You couple that with a shy veneer, then forget about it. The majority of these sensitive's are some of the nicest, friendliest people on the planet when you are in the room with them. They have a deeper understanding than most, which comes with its challenges that include absorbing all of that stimuli.

For those who might not understand why I'm strict about where I go, who I go with, and what time of day I go, then perhaps that can offer some illumination. It may be something that someone else cannot understand unless they have similar strong psychic senses, but in my world it is more real than you can imagine. You may be reading this because you are aware of your psychic gifts and enjoy reading stories about others with a stronger psychic touch, or because you're curious about psychic phenomena, but don't feel you're psychic yourself, although you are more than you may be aware of. I can walk into places that I previously knew would be containing someone or many moving about surrounded by dark souls that will flock to me if I show up, so I have to be hyper vigilante about my surroundings.

Having spent my life to date with one foot in this world and the other in some of the other worlds, my awareness of what's beyond this plane has forever been present. One of them is something rarely mentioned because it's too distasteful and ugly to be believable or entertained. It is the Darkness that exists between this plane and the next. I'm not usually one to shy away from the darkness no matter how horrific or unpleasant it might be to some. This is part of what I had to learn through the ferocious rough and severe upbringing I had coupled with who my soul truly is at its core. Being all love and light is a great quality to have, but you also cannot be naïve to other elements that are alive and affecting a great many souls around the planet.

I've discussed the varying visual accounts of Heaven throughout my life and in several of my books in lavish detail, while only grazing the surface of the Darkness in one of the spirit planes. I've never seen a red Devil with horns or fire everywhere the way it's often portrayed in films, Haunted Houses, and Halloween costumes. It's the same way God isn't some curmudgeon old man with a beard sitting on a chair condemning everyone to blasphemy and Hell if they don't behave themselves.

There is a Darkness that exists that is equitable to the Devil if there were a red ogre with horns and a goatee. This shouldn't be too much of a surprise since the Darkness tends to rule Earth and humanity. This is evident whenever you log online, read comments, or head outside where people congregate.

Every soul is susceptible to the Darkness, including the most enlightened being to ever walk the Earth. No one is exempt or immune from both the Light and Dark elements within yourself or those around you. This is a battle that all souls are challenged with on Earth. There are entities that are more powerful than the Darkness. These include the spirits in Heaven, Archangels, Angels, Saints, Jesus Christ, other higher religious deities, and of course God. Those higher light beings are who you call in to protect you from the Darkness on Earth.

We refer to the beings on the Other Side as Spirits, which makes them sound holographic, opaque, or translucent. This is how they might appear to someone on Earth through Clairvoyance, but they appear as whole as you could possibly imagine on the Other Side. Every single one of them radiates a Light that varies in degrees and color. This is what is seen as attractive on the Other Side in the same way someone might look at a human being and comment that they appear physically attractive, while ignoring their inner character and personality. This is not the case on the Other Side. If a human being is physically good looking and visually appealing on Earth, but their soul is awful or negative in any manner, then on the Other Side their Light would appear dimmer than others. They are not considered as attractive. It's interesting how it's reversed back home.

This isn't to say that there are crummy spirits back home, since everyone is operating on a higher vibration on the Other Side, even if they retain the basic personalities they had on Earth. Those personalities were always a part of them when their soul was made. God made each soul with its own personality and traits.

Dangerous spirits are in one of the dimensions of Hell, which is the dark part of the Spirit World. They can include people that are unaware they are gone, but have avoided moving into the Light. This is where you've likely heard of stories of disturbing spirits or Poltergeist. They are trapped in a perpetual Darkness and still retain their negative qualities and traits. Those negative personality traits aren't wiped away until their soul hits the Light. They have a choice to go into the Light, so no one is preventing them from moving in there. Their consciousness may fear the Light due to the judgment they heard on Earth about it. The resistance they have from allowing the pull of the Light to bring them in is so great they refuse to move. They may be oblivious to the idea that they can move into it just by the thinking, "I want to go into the Light." And they're quickly transported.

When the soul lives in a human body, it gathers up human challenges to build onto that character. The Darkness will battle with the Light to take over that soul and lead it towards destruction, while the Light does its best to stop it. The Light is more powerful than the Dark, but on Earth in this particular plane that is not necessarily the case. The Darkness is its strongest in the contrasting levels of Hell. Since Earth is one of the levels of Hell, although not the worst level believe it or not, the Darkness has more influence. This would be impossible to dispute or debate, because as we've mentioned time and again all you need to do is read the media, social media, YouTube videos, stories, or go to places where more people congregate. Type in your Internet search bar, "Black Friday Violence", and that can give you an eye opener if you don't believe this. Terrorists are not the only people plagued by Darkness. It would also be impossible not to notice the Darkness that plagues so many people unless you reside in a state of naivety or obliviousness, then you won't notice it. If you live off the technical grid in a wide open nature space and connect with a few people if any, then you're lucky in that you may not notice it.

You may also choose to see the good in people, which

is an amazing quality to have, but if you get out there on a daily basis and get into the trenches at one time or another you will be tested to see that this is not the case. God had me go through so many trenches dragged across it, backwards, and forwards that my entire soul consciousness was covered in mud. He did this the way any exceptional warrior soldier is trained. You go to battle for a reason, because He knows you can do it.

The Darkness is one of the different aspects of Hell in the spirit world, rather than the darkness in ourselves, although that is also an important element to be wary of. Sometimes the two can be interconnected.

There may be quite a bit of the love and light stuff being pushed into the ethers in spiritual teachings. Being happy and filled with joy and positivity is a wonderful state to achieve, but ignoring everything else as if it doesn't exist can cause problems too. You cannot fully understand the Light if you don't have an understanding of the Dark. Life is not all cute stuffed animals, flowers, and cuddles.

Having Clairsentience is one of the difficult clair psychic senses to have, because if I see, witness, read, or hear any measure of negativity, then I feel physically ill. There's a sharp pain piercing into my Clairsentience channel and soul. It's not that I don't tolerate bad manners, sensationalized media stories, negativity, political rants, toxic social media posts, or gossip of any kind just because I reside in a state of seemingly self-righteousness that looks down upon it all with disdain. It's that I also receive negative psychic reactions to those kinds of Earthly ego enticements. No one I've communed with in Heaven approves of it. I can feel all of that through my Clairsentience channel when those things happen.

Clairvoyantly seeing both the Light as well as the Darkness has offered me a true eye opener of what's going on out there in the Universe. The Darkness seeps into places around me from the darker part of the spirit worlds, which is one of the levels of Hell. It is no place anyone should want to be in. Depending on who you talk to there have been numerous labels for it such as Hell, Limbo, Purgatory, etc. I've used those words, but more often than not I call it the Darkness, which is the opposite of the Light in the way that Hell is the opposite of Heaven.

CREEPY CRAWLIES

My sporadic and continuous Clairvoyant episodes featuring the fringes of Darkness in the spirit world will reveal pieces of the Darkness puncturing into areas of the Earth plane. When this happens, then I often first see it show up as millions of creepy crawlies spilling into it and moving about on top of one another in a disgusting display that is unfathomable and unimaginable to want to be in. This later explained the etheric incidents as a little kid seeing those creepy crawlies all over my bed and toy box.

The millions of insects start to ooze out of walls, on the sides of buildings, but also on people that have been wallowing or contaminated in the Darkness. That's probably the most disturbing because it initially looks like it's happening through my physical vision. This is to illustrate the intensity of it as best I can. Imagine you're minding your own business and suddenly you see millions of dark creepy insects spilling out and moving about on top of one another in front of you. It looks like they are really there. Envision what your initial reaction will be, because that's what it's like for me.

There is the gasp inhale and the panic upon first seeing it. Through my human vision it looks physically real and as if it's happening in reality. While it is taking place, it's not physically touchable or necessarily harmful to me from Earth. There is a light around me that I've noticed starts to vibrate stronger pulsating in and out when these creepy crawlies and dark elements begin moving towards me, even though when the Darkness is strong enough it can create cuts around my Light to try and get in. The Darkness is doing its best to attack the Light like someone throwing a rock at a window that is strong enough to crack it, but not break it. Cracking it is enough to feel it, so I can't imagine the Light being completely broken, but this is what happens to those that reside in this Darkness. The Darkness has never fully taken me over otherwise that would definitely be noticeable, since I would be doing horrible things to other people from killing and violence. That should answer the question that bad people like that have that Darkness around them. The Darkness is not quite as animated as it was in the film *Ghost*, but the horror of it is intensely bad.

I've sat up in hyper alertness to notice masses of these disgusting insects and creepy crawlies seeping into my room through the corners and down the walls. It truly is one of the grossest things I've ever seen and felt. It initially moves me into a panic that shoots up through my body pushing me into overactive vigilance. Breathe speeds up and eyes widen in horror and shock while I scan all of it through the Clairvoyant part of my third eye vision while sensing a darker predator or more moving in.

The creepy crawlies actually kind of remind me of the *Indiana Jones* films with the insects and snakes, as well as the *Nightmare Before Christmas* when the ghost was unraveled and all of the insects drop to the floor. Although with those fun films it was entertaining, but living it is an entirely different feeling.

When the creepy crawlies are near me, then I know the Darkness is near. The clue to the predator being close is these creepy crawly things start coming out all over the place. They show up first since they're around these predators. It's like when you see birds flocking away abruptly together, then you see the danger come in that they were flocking away from.

I see these creepy crawlies around people that have either been infected by the Darkness or they're fully consumed in the Darkness. I can be walking on the sidewalk behind someone when I see a creepy thing moving around them. This is sometimes followed by the cut and tear on my Light, which is how strong it is. It's enough to make anyone shudder if they saw it in front of them.

When I first see it, it looks real, physical, touchable in front of me as if it's on the Earthly plane. It's only as the clairvoyant vision part of my psychic senses morph in and out of my physical eyes into something less threatening that I can see it changing to translucent, then I've gradually relaxed afterwards. This is knowing that it's real in the dark part of the Spirit world, but I'm protected to an extent. This is the same way I see spirits in my peripheral vision. I often jump with a startle in my daily life because I think it's a human being moving past me or standing there staring. My initial reaction is to jump or grow irritated, because I don't like being watched. After I jump with a startle, then I look again and the image fades in and out from the opaque to translucent and then fades away into a dissolve.

There have been occasions where I've noticed through my Clairvoyance that above me is a gigantic furry Tarantula spider spinning a fast moving web with its legs animatedly moving in harmony as it races downwards towards me like a nasty predator. I've immediately gone into panic, ducked, lowered myself as it's moving closer, then jumped into warrior mode to knock it away. This is before it stops a mere two feet above me unable to get through. I continue ducking and swatting it in a panic. When it stops just before it hits me it fades away, but oh my the panic induced is ridiculous. I've abruptly raced away down the sidewalk, out of a room, or a house I'm in. People see me swatting something they can't see. Now imagine how crazy that must appear to onlookers. I've been on high alert knocking chairs and furniture over when it happens suddenly. I've had friends catch these incidents and get startled because they see me shadow boxing something they can't see. It evaporates and starts to seep in and out and I realize it's a psychic vision. I quickly calm down and stand there feeling super lame for a second.

At times while knocking some of these crawlies away, I can see through my left peripheral vision the gigantic pockets of creepy crawlies seeping in different areas around them, so everything starts to happen at once. It's not like the spider glides down alone. It slides down at the same time the others are racing out to attack. They often start to pour out of corners especially since Darkness can get lodged and stuck in those areas. This is also why some people will Sage corners of rooms more than other areas, since corners are a draw for dark energy that can get lodged in there.

I've gone back into the room to see that it's gone. I'm

suspicious looking around.

"It was just here, where the Hell did that thing go?"

I then gasp seeing the pockets of these creepy crawlies moving down the walls again as I slowly back away, then they evaporate and I realize, "Wait a minute, this is not actually here."

I scope the area again moving my grouchy concerned face closer to the wall and I see it moving from physical to translucent, and I realize it's etheric. You'd think after enough of these encounters for decades that you would get used to it, but you never truly do because of how sudden it happens and how gross it looks.

Growing up, this was how I learned it was coming through from the darker part of the spirit world. It's the brilliance of the Light and Heaven that is often talked about, but neglected are the discussions of the Darkness in the other planes. Becoming trapped in that horror is no place for any soul. This has been the same way prophetic visions that have later come true for me come in. It comes through one of my psychic clair senses in my soul, as if it's happening in front of me. It can take a minute before I realize it's just a vision.

On other occasions when the Darkness has infected me and I didn't notice it right away, I then have to sometimes re-trace my steps that day to see who was infected that I might have come across, because the Darkness is drawn to that. It means it latched onto me in a different way beyond the cutting and stayed with me.

I've lived in beach cities for more than half of my life, but there was a period when I chose to take myself out of my element and live in the trenches of Hollywood, California between 2011-2014. When I was living in the city of Hollywood, the creepy crawly things were massive and everywhere. I couldn't believe how infected the city of Hollywood was by it. A best friend once commented,

"That's not hard to believe."

We have a telepathic shorthand that I already knew what he meant. Because there are so many souls in Hollywood that are detached from the Light due to not believing in it or due to the abundant amount of toxic choices, thoughts, and feelings that go on there, then it's safe to assume that they are attracting this Darkness in on a much larger scale than in other cities. There is quite a bit of souls in that city that are spiritually corrupt or spiritually bankrupt. They are either lovers of self to the extreme as far as you can get, or they are internally damaged that they fill themselves up with drug, alcohol, or any other toxic vice they can get their hands onto as a replacement for the Light. This is what I did in my early twenties and there was so much Darkness around me during that time. It seemed impossible to get me out of it once I was there, but my Spirit team did repeatedly fight hard to pull me out.

Long after I moved back to the beach, I went to Hollywood for a visit as I hadn't been there in awhile. I was stunned at how dramatically it changed in the years since I left. It had grown more congested and packed. The streets were a parking lot of cars that weren't moving. People were agitated, angry, rushed, and unfocused. Those states of being are impossible for spiritual psychic focus. While driving I noticed there was a guy on the sidewalk on his stomach having convulsions, which I knew was from consuming drugs. There were about ten to fifteen people standing around, since it was also next to a bus stop, but not one person ran to his aid. Those closest to him stepped away or looked away pretending it wasn't happening as if they couldn't be bothered. You can bet that in a smaller town everyone would have ran over to help him. I skidded my car to the side and raced over while calling the Paramedics with my other hand, then everyone kind of moved in slightly while being hesitant. You have to ask yourself in those situations, "What would Jesus do?"

This isn't just in Hollywood, California that is bathed in the most Darkness. Many sections of Southern California are like that and in other parts of the world, especially where you have an overcrowded situation. The Darkness is attracted in seeing it as a feeding ground so to speak. The worse I personally saw it was in Hollywood, but I can say that since I'm a Southern California native. I've had discussions about this later in life with those in Southern California and in Hollywood and they've quickly chimed in to agree and share their personal stories about it. Although more than half my life has been in beach cities, which is mostly relaxed and chill than moving into the deeper parts of the big bad city. There are still people plagued with Darkness there too, since they are all over the planet. It's not as massive as I experienced it while in Hollywood though.

The Darkness shows up predominately in areas where tons of people are since they're the most susceptible to pulling the Darkness in due to how erratic their emotional well-being states fluctuate. It's challenging to get centered in a packed city. There are scientific studies that have shown how it adds stress and anxiety to ones health and well-being. It's that state that drops your vibration and makes you a magnet for the Darkness to drink that up. It's drawn and pulled in to someone that has a lower energy and begins to feed off them like a vampire. The Darkness can prompt people to spiral into more negativity, since its goal is domination and destruction.

If you are in tune and aware of it, then you can easily get rid of it by calling in the Light. That is one of the other numerous benefits to being psychically in tune. You know when there is danger or darkness near and you can easily call in the Archangel Michael and your Spirit team to intervene. You follow this by examining what it is that is happening in your life that is on the severe negative or toxic side that could bring in something like that to you. You can feel it since it affects your overall well-being state, so that's a good indication that you have these cuts being made as well too.

One of the more heartbreaking views is when I see someone with no Light around them at all, but a complete Darkness infestation. Those tend to be people that are violent, full of hate, bullying, and/or heavily addicted to some kind of toxic vice. People that reside in a perpetual daily negative state are Darkness magnets without realizing it. Go to a social media account and if you see someone's page filled with non-stop negativity or gossipy related posts, then you can be sure that they have been infected by the Darkness in an impressive way that it has taken over them. That person has become a pawn puppet that is being commanded by the Darkness without them even realizing it. They're so far removed from any positivity and light that they have complete amnesia of being taken over, because the Darkness will put a blindfold on you once it gets a hold of you.

There are gifted people that can pick up on this Darkness as well if they have strong Clairvoyance or a keen Clairsentience channel. Some may see these things while in a lucid dreaming state. This is because the main part of your conscious is asleep, which helps in removing those blocks that would prevent you from seeing it while in a waking state. Some of those things in the dream are real, but just in another plane seeping into this plane, while other things in the dream are your subconscious.

It is physically and spiritually painful for the soul to be around dark energy. The one giving off that dark energy will soon find it manifests into more. This causes them to drop into that energy becoming one with it. It's a breeding ground for far worse illnesses that can come about at some point in their life. This is not the only factor that determines an illness though, but it is one of them.

It mind boggles me to see others residing in that state, because I wonder can't they feel that? Is that perpetual negative feeling enjoyable? How exhausting to be planted in an indefinite miserable well-being state and never try anything to change that.

I have come across people that have been attacked by the Darkness and have been so far gone until their Spirit team brings them a breakthrough that prompts the person to receive that a-ha moment. Some of those falling into the Darkness have approached me and said, "I know things aren't right with me and I want to change it, but I don't know how."

Right there is the awakening moment and the first step to spiritual recovery. It is the first step that shows this particular person is capable and ready to evolve. They have admitted that the way things have been going for them for years in that negativity state no longer works for them. It has drained their life force that they have no more energy to continue. It is too heavy on the soul to continue that way and they have grown conscious and aware of it. They want to change and through that admitting and being aware of it, they have graduated to the next step where the real work comes in.

CHAPTER FOUR

Earth Angels,

Spirit Guides and Angels,

and the Soul Contract

Lucifer was a fallen angel that once resided in Heaven. He was magnificently beautiful looking and made this incredible music sound wherever he moved. One day he decided to defy the Light in a big way and was cast out of Heaven due to the corruption he was attempting to create. It's important to note that he chose to be cast out. He had that choice because God doesn't keep any prisoners or anyone that doesn't want to be there, regardless if it's an angel or human being. We're not puppets on strings that God is playing and controlling.

All souls have free will choice to do something good or choose to do something bad. Lucifer made the latter choice time and again that his soul was drawn out of Heaven since the Light spits that stuff out if it's contaminated. He fell like a lightning bolt and now resides in what some refer to as a fiery pit of Hell. Some belief systems believe there is this fiery pit with Lucifer looking like a red ogre with a tail and pitchfork that has become a popular culture image, especially during Halloween time and in scary films. This is not what he looks like as he's quite exceptionally beautiful looking, but his soul is hideously dangerous. This is how he can cause such deception to the ego mind, because the ego is pulled in by someone's attractive exterior instead of what's in the soul's heart.

As mentioned earlier, Earth is one of the dimensions of Hell. This means that Lucifer is not actually below the Earth, but here on Earth. He is technically located in one of the layers of Hell located between Earth and Heaven. This is one of the additional explanations of why I have seen these creepy crawlies and other darker entities spilling into the Earth plane since childhood. I could never understand that throughout my adolescence until the missing pieces to the puzzle were being shown to me by my Spirit team over the course of time. Then I was mesmerized as if I had discovered gold, "Ohhhhhh. Wow. That's interesting."

Lucifer is close enough to create destruction in the lives of human beings. He does this because he can. He wants power the way some human beings desire greed and power. It isn't for the purpose of good, but the purpose of annihilation and ruin. He works through them to push them to accomplish this through simple manipulation and influence. It's like taking candy from a baby it's so easy. Earth is owned by God, but the Devil is temporarily running it by infecting anyone he can. It's not just through vitriolic hatred and violence, but he can do this through selfishness, greed, and self-centeredness. He invades people's minds by poisoning it. He can do little deceptive things such as whispering into your consciousness that you're no good at anything. He'll crush your self-esteem, because he enjoys belittling and bullying others. He'll also do that through other people by contaminating and influencing them to behave badly with others. These are the ones that are predominately bad, rather than the rare moment a genuinely good person is stressed out about something. Examine how many people believe the negative thoughts about themselves. No Light being will ever talk to you the way the Darkness does. The Devil will steal souls to create a growing army of Darkness in the Hell regions, including on Earth which is evident. Your soul can choose to live in the Light which will take that power away from the Darkness. The most difficult ones he can't get into easily are those of the Light on Earth.

Earth is one of Lucifer's dominions where he has some of the most success at rallying, enslaving, and masterfully manipulating millions of souls every second all at once. He plagues the planet by working through them. They form into Locusts that spread and urinate lower energy wherever possible. To counter that God sends His trusty light warriors to contribute their parts at tempering and stomping that darkness out as much as possible. We sometimes call these lights Earth Angels that incarnate from another land beyond the veil, but even they can be susceptible to the lower energy if they're not careful. They are gifted and capable of wiping it away as quickly as possible and getting right back to work with their exceptionally keen focus, drive, and purpose. God only sends His best, which only angers the Darkness like you would never believe. God's best are a thorn in the side of the Darkness.

The Light warriors tend to be highly sensitive in some way, as well as profoundly psychic more than those that are unaware of their psychic abilities. They are more in-tune to the vibrations beyond the physical plane due to the many previous life lessons they've gained. The harder the life lesson the stronger your evolving process is. The more you evolve the clearer your consciousness. The clearer your consciousness the keener your psychic channels are.

The Light souls on Earth do their best to stay away from anyone that resides in a lower energy space. They can detect when to steer clear due to having a vastly tuned-in calibrated psychic antennae. They move towards those that reside in a higher vibrational Light state, while the darker human soul attracts in others that reside in a negative space. Their negative energy grows more repressed as the Dark energies take over, while the stronger sensitive soul rises like helium above the Darkness and into the vortex of the Light where love resides.

One of the few traits that all Earth Angels have in common is that they're keenly aware they are here to do His will. This is the common link that brings them all together in a communal circle like the Avengers fighting crime. Each brings their distinctive personalities and talents to their holy rampage with the goal of protecting and progressing humanity and the planet.

Some higher evolved souls will continue to incarnate into an Earthly life beyond their final incarnation. They are not doing that for the purpose of balancing out any Karmic debt or for soul growth purposes, even though the positive side effect is additional soul growth. This is never shunned by an intelligent consciousness. They desire to contribute something positive towards humanity that can benefit the planet.

Many of the higher evolved souls are the warriors of lights, light workers, and earth angels that all view the planet as God's home and creation that needs protection. It's similar to when someone housesits for a best friend. They treat the home as if it is their own. Because they are protectors of His work, they have a deep desire to keep the planet healthy on His behalf. Relying on newborn souls to keep it in great shape is not an option, because when you put a tantrum havoc-wreaking child in a room, then you cannot expect it to clean that room up. You might walk into that room to find it is in complete disarray with crayon writing on the wall.

The child needs to be trained and taught that destroying a room is not appropriate behavior. The child that resists knowledge ends up having a harder life. Every soul on the planet has the soul capacity for great knowledge gained including the tantrum child. They need higher evolved souls or evolving souls to guide and teach them. We see these higher evolved souls in the people around the world that are making some kind of positive difference in the lives of human beings. Some of these highly evolved souls may not even be cognizant of their role. They enjoy what they do so much that the deeper meaning and quest behind what they're doing isn't on their radar.

It is easier for a higher evolved soul to accomplish those tasks while in a human body, rather than attempting to do it in a spirit body that many don't pay attention to. Most people either have trouble accessing God, Spirit, the Angels, Higher Spirit Beings, or they don't believe in it. Irrespective of anyone's personal human belief system this lifetime, every soul has the gifts of Divine communication.

Higher evolved souls view the constant chaos on Earth from Heaven as all souls do through the veil. Gradually some of them come to the conclusion that they must incarnate into a human body for a specific cause that can help progress Earthly life positively in some way. If the higher evolved souls never choose to come to Earth, then Earth will eventually be destroyed. It's similar to the abandoned home that is soon ruined and destroyed by trespassers that have no consciousness. If you think Earth is in a poor state now, then imagine if the souls of the Light that are here now trying to temper that decided not to come here. Earthly life would end up in ruins and completely destroyed. Things like there would be no human laws enacted to capture criminals and keep them locked up to prevent further destruction. Even though it is true some of the laws are warped and criminalize people that are not truly criminals. They might have committed a crime that would be considered minor in Heaven's eyes, as opposed to a larger true crime such as grand theft, murder, assault, or physical harm and violence to another person or property.

The danger for the higher evolved soul that incarnates into a human life is they are as susceptible to the negative energies as anyone else. They can succumb too deeply to Earthly pleasures that could prevent them from getting to work. I know this well since my spirit has experienced everything under the sun, around the block, and back again. Keeping it balanced is significant to guarantee you don't get lost in it to the point that months have passed by and you realize, "Wait a minute I haven't accomplished anything good."

That was a statement I had made during my adolescent stage more than once. This doesn't mean I was never exempt from behaving what some might consider badly. I grew up this lifetime as a rebellious reckless aggressive warrior soul. Wanting to get my hands onto anything that was toxic. Temptations have never been beneath me in the past. If I had never tried it before, then I wanted to. Some of it was for me to escape the pain I was experiencing in this life due to the repetitive childhood trauma, but some of it was also to experience so that I could have a better understanding of it and report back. All the colors on my souls palette were bright and receptive to it all. At the same time I was fearless despite all the warnings of those around me that I shouldn't do certain things. If I shouldn't do it, then I would.

I remember a sixty-something year old man informed me that people would get drunk or high on cough syrup when he was growing up, but only with the boxes that had the warning label that said, "May be habit forming."

So what did I do? Caroused the aisles at the local drug store with a friend of mine until I found the cough syrup section. I stood there strong, and persistent, while impatiently and angrily flipping around each and every box. My perplexed friend that accompanied me said, "What are you looking for?"

I slammed in, "Alcohol."

That's an example of an addict, an insatiable curiosity, or both, which I was all of the above and much more. I may be highly in tune, but I'm also a former addict to anything and everything I could get my hands onto. Our human lives are always met with some measure of turmoil. Even the ones you think who have everything down or who have it together are not exempt from this. They also have lessons they're wrestling with since no one gets a free pass.

The higher evolved soul may choose to incarnate for a specific purpose that contributes something awesome to human life. As long as they're going to take the time to incarnate and live a human life to be able to accomplish this, they will add other elements in their soul contract to achieve while at it. They might choose to live a harder life for a brief period that will help their soul adapt to the harsher aspects of Earthly life. This way they can gain important disciplined traits they need to help them accomplish their purpose or purposes. The soul is aware before incarnating that the risk of their Earthly mission is that their soul's memories of Heaven and their psychic channels will be suppressed and potentially diminished once in a human body. This is why many human beings tend to have amnesia about where their soul came from or what it's like back home in Heaven.

Over time there will be souls on Earth that begin to remember or discover ways that can help re-open their psychic channels they're born with. I've talked about many of those methods throughout my work. Much of what my Spirit team has filtered through me to discuss isn't to ruin someone's Earthly pleasurable fun or to condemn troublesome behavior that can backfire on you. It's to offer what helps in awakening those psychic clair senses that is more connected to God than anything else. Having a strong faith based system makes life a bit easier than not having that faith. God is your long-term family unit and you want Him on your side. Everything my Spirit team teaches is also for me too. I'm certainly not exempt from this. During my adolescent immature phase, I disregarded what they'd teach the way any teenager scoffs and disregards what their own parents are attempting to instill in them. As I was growing older I was still aware of what my Spirit team had been teaching me and was beginning to adopt much of what they had been teaching. I realized what they were helping me with was on the mark, so I began to share that with others that were interested too.

SPIRIT GUIDES AND ANGELS

In order to easily access God, He gives each soul at least one main Spirit Guide and one Guardian Angel to assist and guide where needed throughout your Earthly life. Communicating with your Guide and Angel is communicating with God despite what some might feel about the matter. They are His hands and arms so you are communicating with Him. Your Guide and Angel are with you from your human birth until your human death. Before you are born into an Earthly life, you commune with your Spirit team that consists of one Guide and one Angel.

It's your Guardian Angel that will be there for you during the moments when emotional healing is needed. Your Spirit Guide works with you on the practical survival stuff. For instance, your upset about a break up that happened or the death of a loved one, then your angel comes to your side. You're having trouble finding a job, a new apartment/home, or relationship, then your Spirit Guide would help with that. It's not that cut and dry, since they both work overtime on guiding you over little day to day things too, but this is more or less what their roles tend to be like.

A person's Guardian Angel and Spirit Guide are always near the person they're assigned to in many ways on varying levels. Being connected to them is like having a best friend in another dimension. Like God, these are beings that know everything about you, all of the good and the bad. They know your thoughts and feelings, the things you hide, the things you reveal, and yet they never leave your side. They continue to love you unconditionally no matter how horrific a human crime you've done, which isn't saying that you won't need to pay for that crime depending on the severity. One of their jobs is to support and guide you on the right path. This includes through paying for karma created. When you act out and cause trouble in school, then you're sent to the principles office to be disciplined. The soul class works in a similar way, but some of the soul crimes are not all the same as the Earthly crimes. If you're headed towards danger, then they do their best to stop you or steer you away from that. This is why it's important to be clear minded and to develop a strong connection with them. It helps you decipher between a good decision and a bad one when you're tuned in to them daily.

Many are aware that everyone has one main spirit guide and one guardian angel that is with you from the moment you're born in a human body to the moment you depart that human body. If you haven't seen them through Clairvoyance throughout your Earthly life, then when you cross over back home you most definitely will see them in front of you as clear as the day. You will instantly know them like running into a friend you hadn't seen in awhile. This realization is immediate and automatic.

When one talks about you having one main spirit guide and guardian angel, what is often left out is how are they with you from human birth and human death? What if someone is a couch potato that sits and watches trash television all day, then gossips on the phone when there is another lull? Is this magnificent Spirit Guide and Guardian Angel hanging around on the couch with that person? I don't know about you, but I'd slit my wrists if I was stuck guiding someone like that. In spiritual reality, I wouldn't feel like a failure that I'm unable to reach that person at all throughout their life, because feelings like failure are non-existent on the Other Side. You just keep trying to get that person's attention repeatedly throughout their life and hope for the best.

The Spirit Guide and Guardian Angel are with the soul in the human body they've soul contractually agreed to be with, stand by, and guide. They are not hanging around the person 24/7 for decades or however long that particular person lives. The guide and angel have other things they are doing on the Other Side. They are alerted to oncoming danger before it takes place, because their psychic foresight is at the 100% mark. They know all before anyone does or says anything the same way God does. They can see the projected outcome of this circumstance coming in before it happens. They can then guide the soul away from that danger. There is never an incident where a Spirit Guide or Guardian Angel is late to an incident. It's impossible due to their psychic radar and the incredible access they have to that person's complicating and intricate soul records. They know what's about to take place. If a person is operating with free will, which many tend to do, and they're heading for danger, the guide and angel are alerted way in advance of a probable outcome that's about to happen, so they have plenty of time to warn the person. At that point, they can only hope that the person is tuned in enough to pick up on those warnings.

One of the benefits of being in constant communication with God and your Spirit team is that they become a part of your daily life. When you are talking to them about an issue that's popped up that someone else did that affected you, they are already there and present to help you do something about it so that you can move on from it and onto more important things.

My mother recalled a story when I was eight years old and accompanied her at the local mall. I walked away from her independently as I tend to still do today with everyone it seems. She was looking around to see where I went and found me staring at this shelf filled with angel statues. She said she remembers I had a furious expression on my face. Perplexed while watching me turn towards her angrily shouting while pointing to the statues, "Why are they all blonde with wings?! That's not how they look!"

Ah, the injustice was boiling the inner waters of this warrior soul to a furious rage. That's because the depiction of angels in artwork has forever presented angels in a manner that is inaccurate to what they truly look like, but instead in a way that is more comfortable for people to accept.

One of the other things that would cause a sneer is that guardian angel depictions are usually cutesy cherub little fluffy angels. It's no wonder there are so many skeptics, because no reasonable and rational person could possibly believe they look like cute cuddly stuffed animals. There are cherub looking angels on the Other Side, but they deal more with matters of love, and they are far from cuddly. I'm thinking of the Munchkins in the Wizard of Oz. Ferocious with grand reasonable personalities.

For centuries, there have been countless stories of people encountering an angel in physical form. This is from both believers and non-believers alike. They've been recounted in every holy book in every religion known to man. Regardless of someone's personal belief system, nearly 80% of the planet has a strong belief in angels even if they're not religious. That's every 8 out of 10 people. This is because when they encounter one on those rare occasions there is no doubt. Many that have had angel encounters protested to not believing "in any of that". This changed after the encounter that was deep and profound enough that it altered their conscious perception. Many have experienced similar encounters with an angel especially during traumatic or dire circumstances. Those are the venues where an angel makes its presence known. Angels tend to show up as the person needs it. It's those little reminders that tell you that you are not alone.

Angels show up and hear your prayers and remain present during a time that it's most needed, especially for those with rapidly failing health. When it's someone's time to go back home to Heaven, then the angels and that person's Spirit team along with other beings from Heaven are standing around that person working double time. It's kind of like when an entire family goes to pick someone up at the airport and arrives just before the person has landed. You're standing around waiting for their arrival to pick them up and take them with you. There is often more than one spirit being waiting along with the Archangel Azrael, the angel of death, which is not as cryptic as that sounds. If the person is in the hospital, but has three months to live, then in addition to that persons Spirit team being present throughout, deceased relatives begin flocking within the last number of days as well too.

Angels don't have eyes, as creepy as that might sound to imagine, because we're used to everyone having eyes. They also don't have an anatomy. Even though paintings of angels show them as looking like human beings. In movies they're made to look like us, so everyone thinks or believes they look like a man or a woman.

Angels are a magnificent bright light source created out of God's fire to act as His trusty strong and compassionate assistants. Like all beings, angels can and do morph into the appearance of something human. When they do morph into a human being, their eyes are one of the first initial ways to recognize them, because their eyes, which can be any color, are striking and pierce through you.

When people have had angel encounters, they know without a doubt that it was an angel regardless of how it appeared.

My mother once asked, "Where do you get your great sense of humor? It can't be from any of us."

I said without hesitation, "From the Angels."

Because contrary to some beliefs about Heaven being this cold dark place where judgment occurs, they tend to exude traits of joy, humor, and laughter. When you spend enough time with them, then it will rub off on you as it does with me.

SOUL CONTRACT

Before you have an Earthly life, your soul got together with a council of highly evolved heavenly leaders that work with you to put a soul contract together. The soul contract includes many of the main events that will happen in your life and the reasons for those events. The many soul mates you'll encounter will also be listed along with the estimated dates that they show up. Everything in the soul contract is a forecasted estimation, because you are also granted free will choice to do what you want to do. Paying attention to God and your Spirit team helps you fulfill your destinies in this contract. You ask for their help when needed, you follow their guidance, and take action when necessary.

When you ignore God and your Spirit team, and you ignore what's in your contract, then they will repeatedly put up the same sign to get you to notice it in hopes you'll take action on it. If you continue to ignore it, then that same sign will continue as long as it needs to. For some people the same sign never goes away. When the person reaches senior age or their final years they might come to the conclusion that there were things they were supposed to do, but they never did. Those things were in their souls contract, but they ignored it and chose to set out to have a different life. They realize when they arrive back home all of the things that were contracted and what they accomplished from it and what they didn't. This is also part of the reason why the soul develops amnesia when they incarnate into a human body. Part of that is for their protection. If they knew exactly what was to take place, then they would never live life. They would sit around and wait for it to happen.

If the soul sits around waiting for the contracted events to take place, they would waste their time because the events would not happen due to their free will choice to sit and wait for it. The soul has many purposes it needs to set out to do while here. Each human soul is given just enough information from Spirit at the right time that is allowed on God's timing. Even the most psychic person on the planet won't be able to see everything. They can only see what God allows them to see at that moment, which can come through in psychic snippets and flashes.

When the contract is drawn up in Heaven, also listed

is that there will be different special guides or angels that will show up temporarily to help the soul with pivotal events, such as getting the right job, finding the right soul mate partner, and on up to greater quests that help humanity in a positive way.

What is also drawn out and included in this lengthy soul contract that can fill a book are the experiences you agree to endure in that Earthly lifetime. This includes your life purpose, goals, lessons, missions, and the challenges you will face. There are various bullet points listed that assist in the growth and evolvement of your soul. Also, included in this contract are the soul mates and karmic connections you will meet along your journey. These relationships are intended to assist in expanding and growing your soul. They include family members, friendships, colleagues, acquaintances, and lovers. They make up the many soul mates you encounter in your life.

You are also set up with three separate departure times throughout your Earthly lifetime. If the first two points of Earthly departure are denied and decided against, then the third departure time is the Earthly death. It is the maximum allowable time you've agreed upon in living one Earthly life. You might even recall one or two previous moments where you almost died for good. These are the not same as near death experiences which are enacted to awaken the soul that needs to be awakened for a greater purpose.

Your soul contract is in a personal book devoted to you that the Archangel Metatron keeps that some call the Akashic Records. There are key circumstances that are listed to take place in it, but that doesn't mean every single one of those bullet points will happen. Things like free will choice can delay or negate it all together. For example, in the book it might state that you'll meet a love partner at age twenty-eight. It describes who that person is and other details about them as well as where and when you'll meet them. Due to free will choice and other unforeseen circumstances beyond your control or this other person's control, delays can push it out, then you find that you end up meeting this person at age thirty-six. The delays or free will choices pushed the circumstance further out, while in other cases delays and free will choices are so great that it pushes it out indefinitely. The path crossing with this person never happens or it comes so close, but you both miss it.

All human souls have the capacity to see, feel, know, and hear messages and guidance from beyond. Everyone is equally and unequivocally psychic for the purpose of being able to connect with their Spirit team. You're on a mission on Earth and they are guiding you in that mission. If you are not picking up on anything psychically, then that means you are experiencing a block. Blocks form easily in the physical Earthly life since the physical life is a challenging one. Human beings generate most of the problems that exist. If there were no human beings on the planet, then the planet's energy life force would evolve and re-grow itself on its own without the tampering destruction that people tend to wreak on it.

CHAPTER FIVE

A Warrior Is Born

Being a lifelong psychic is why my faith has remained consistent. Conversing with Heaven through my keen psychic senses for so long is the reason I believe in it. I've sometimes vaguely heard there are those that have no understanding of spirit communication. The generic retort is that you're not supposed to talk to angels or guides. The ignorance in those statements reveals someone that is not an expert in Heaven, so it's not something I pay attention to or follow. It's like an Animal Veterinarian telling a Surgeon how not to operate on a human patient. You stick with what you're qualified at and I'll focus on what I'm qualified at.

I don't pray to angels or guides, since I give all glory to God. The Angels and Archangels are God's hands and arms, which means they are extensions of God. They have never been human, even though they can appear human if they choose. The only exceptions are Archangel Metatron and Archangel Sandalphon, who were special cases in that they were human at one time, but God morphed them into Archangels because He chose to. Communicating with an Angel or Archangel is communicating with God. Regardless who you are choosing to communicate with, God is hearing it whether you want Him to or not. You might be communicating with a dangerous presence, but God hears that too. He and your Spirit team will try and intervene, which can be picked up on when your psychic senses are highly tuned in.

I was never trained to call on the Angels, Archangels, or Guides for that matter, nor do I practice yoga or meditate, not that I have any problem with anyone that does, because I have many friends in the spiritual communities that do. We all respect our own ways of doing things with love and without judgment. As a restless driven warrior soldier, my souls physical energy charges forward with more energy than those decades younger than I. It's always been like that and hasn't stopped yet, but this restless fighter soul energy is infused into the human part of me. This makes it challenging for me to sit still and meditate or do yoga exercises, because it's not how my soul was made. When I'm in nature I may sit or lie down for awhile to kick back and absorb God's uplifting healing energy for a bit, then I'll stroll on foot to breathe it all in. This is how I personally connect, but what works for me may not work for you. You may already have your own way of doing things or this might offer you ideas on how to connect on your own.

Heavenly guides and angels were already coming in and communicating with me since childhood. A four year old doesn't know to call in a team of Guides and Angels, so you cannot fault a child for his communications that were happening on their own without me doing anything. I was minding my own business playing outside and I heard them. Since then, my Spirit team has been excellently guiding me over the years towards salvation and accomplishment enough for me to know their goal is to keep me on the path of working for God as one of His warriors of lights. It's not a job I can do alone while on Earth due to the compressed density of this plane with the constant Darkness emanating out of so many human souls.

There have been more than enough psychic phenomena happenings within my own life since childhood to know they are not demons. I know the difference between demonic and angelic energy. It is true that a demon entity can disguise itself as an angel to deceive someone, but most clear souls on Earth would know the difference by how the end result is. If you're being guided to fame and fortune, then you can be sure it's not an angelic presence guiding you. If you're guided to creative self expression that ultimately helps others, then that would be an angelic presence. Any fame or fortune that happens to come out of that is merely the side effect to God's work you're doing on Earth. Fame to me is more of a negative side effect, but the monetary increase with that is a positive side effect if it's keeping you employed enough to continue doing what you love without worry of not being able to physically survive on the planet.

The demonic entities and Darkness did its best to keep me in child abuse for so long, pushed me to do drugs and alcohol, and pushed me to do other bad things I've done in the past, which we can attribute the latter to rebellious adolescence as well. The demon Darkness was not pushing me to succeed and be the best I can be or to help me continuously change, thrive, and evolve. It was not present in working through me to get me experience in my first retail job, to the success working with many notables in the film industry. All of that experience was in order to prepare me to write books that teach concepts in the areas of metaphysical, spiritual, parapsychology, and philosophy. The books didn't happen until God and my Spirit team knew I was ready. They knew the life lessons were gained by being dragged through an extreme amount of trenches, then I rose up into the grand work experience that brought out more of the warrior like confidence. The serious long-term love relationships I've endured also added additional challenges and lessons. All of those were lessons gained that would be applied to the bigger work coming up. What you're working on now is the class you're taking that you'll eventually graduate from to move to the next level. You'll take those tools learned and utilize them in your next chapter.

God and my Spirit team council family are the reasons I believe and have continued faith. Sure there have been rare moments my faith has waned on occasion. Working so hard and seeing little return could make anyone want to quit. Or working so hard that you're just exhausted and don't want to keep going as you don't see the point. I've then exclaimed to God and my Spirit team that I'm quitting, I've had it, and I'm done! I've heard them mumble with unimpressed casual nonchalance by my dramatics, "Really?" They have this tone that says, "Yeah, right."

As they've informed me during those moments time and again, "The only time you've truly needed us to the gravest degree is when you're threatening to quit."

They'll add things like, "You've been doing great this whole time more than you know. We haven't had to maneuver much for you because you're doing it. It's only when you break and cower down and offer threats of quitting and walking away from it all do we have to step back in and lift you back up to God. This is where you were before you fell to your knees in despair. We say rise up child and keep going."

One of the big phrases they've never stopped telling me is, "Don't forget who you are."

They know that phrase has immense power, because it suddenly transports my soul back home to the physical warrior God made me in Heaven to be. I then see me back home again working and functioning effortlessly in my role realizing that who I am in this life is barely a sliver of that magnificence. Your true soul from back home resides deep inside your current consciousness with barely a smidge of its presence shining through in random blips. The words, "Don't forget who you are", is the repetitive mantra that floats through my mind, and then I rise back up and move bravely onward again.

There are millions of little moments throughout my life when I'm constantly reminded of how blessed I am. When I feel the power of Him strong enough to touch me, then my eyes flood with that rare emotion of gratitude as my spiritual sight sifts back over all of the endless years of struggle to the contentment I've predominately been in. My life has been one battle after another. Grew up in poverty, was physically, verbally, and psychologically abused repetitively throughout my childhood and into the teenage years by my father. It was a nightmare that I could never wake up from. The only chance of waking up from it was in going to sleep and Clairvoyantly dreaming. This way I was able to see who I am and not this child that was living under violent repressed oppression on Earth. By the time I was eight years old, I started to refer to my father as the Devil, because only a Devil has the power to be a monster on Earth. For me to be truthful about that, my past, and everything I've ever written, it's also to say that you're not alone if you've suffered. I understand because I've been through it too. Eventually I broke away from the abuse, but moved right into the drug and alcohol addiction to cope and endure until the Light guided me out of the Darkness in my early twenties and started to bless me in major ways.

Something like that would break most people. When it broke me, it would only do so for a minute or two, but then I'd be lifted back up. God would reappear refusing to allow me to be broken down by any of the poor human circumstances I was stuck in at the time. He loved and strengthened me back to life and into complete spiritual centeredness. Every day when I wake up from sleep, it's always felt like a new dawn where I'm renewed again. This is regardless of what my state was in the day before. If it was a bad day the day before, then I pray, go to bed, I wake up fully healed and restored with an optimistic attitude ready and revved to go again. To this day, I still converse with God and my Spirit team each morning.

I ask, "What should we accomplish today?"

Because I don't like wasting a day not knowing what needs to be done. There isn't a day that goes by that I don't wake up without asking that question. I'm not into slacking, watching television, or reading gossip stories. I enjoy being productive while squeezing in fun time here and there as well to re-charge and keep the balance.

I've had a hard life and my faith has remained strong even during those massively difficult tumultuous times. As I've grown older those difficult times were gradually growing less severe. This doesn't mean I'm fully exempt from tough challenging times. Challenging times still arise once in awhile such as through the day to day logistics of doing the work I do or other curve balls that fly at me, but it's not as severe as the traumatic child abuse or the drug and alcohol addictions I was once residing in. Knowing without a doubt that God will come through for me keeps me going, because He has when I've asked. It's not always right away no matter how much I ask for particular blessings or assistance with something. There may be a delay depending on what it is.

A child repeatedly asks his parent for a toy. The parent continuously replies, "Not right now."

If the child continued to ask, then a strong parent won't be bullied into submission to buy the toy so the child would stop asking. The parent continues to delay getting that toy until one day when the child has forgot all about it or stops asking, then he's rewarded with the toy. This is similar to how God works. Once you've let go of the frustrated need to obtain a desire, then do the blessings start to filter in. Think of a strong task master disciplinarian parent and you'll get a feeling for what God is like. This strong task master disciplinarian trait should not be confused with abuse.

Wise Ones are often some of the world's greater teachers. They are efficient in governing their students through disciplined rules and action. They are not hard for the sake of it, but because they have a grander purpose for you. They know you cannot grow unless you endure challenging times. God and Wise One souls will sit back as you live through particular challenges before the rewards come in. They offer the rewards and blessings when they know you are in a position to receive it in the right spirit. If you're handed blessings and gifts right away, then it isn't long before you squander or take advantage of that. It has made others behave in a spoiled entitled manner expecting everything to be given if they throw a tantrum.

This is sometimes seen in some of the circles where money is easy to come by. There are good and bad people in all brackets. I have a great many friends that have money, but it hasn't gone to their heads. I've also witnessed people of money who will throw a tantrum and wield that power in order to get what they want. It's the latter folks were talking about to illustrate an example of someone who is used to receiving blessings. What happens when a blessing isn't being immediately granted or they're not getting what they want? They throw a fit on someone and bully them until they get it.

There is a Divine plan for all souls, especially when it is challenging to believe that. I've had to learn the hard way in how He works on His timing. One needs to learn to stop asking for things that you're not ready for. The Universe, God, Spirit is not going to give you everything you ask for the second you ask for it. No one is going to be given something before they're spiritually ready for it. You might think you are, but when you are then it is given. This is similar to how you wouldn't hand a ten year old the keys to your car. It's because you know they're not ready to drive yet. He works on His time and not anyone else's.

STAY CENTERED GURU

God eventually does come through in better ways than you can imagine. I didn't grow up in a religious household. Believe me if anyone else had endured the dangerous circumstances I lived through one after the other, then that would give them reason enough to lose it and it has. Having been raised in a violent abusive household with parents that struggled with money adds to the differing perception of human life than those growing up in a less dysfunctional environment. Growing up not loved by any human being gave me an enlightening lesson. I didn't need to be loved by anyone, because the love I was getting from above was stronger, loyal, long lasting, and more powerful than any human being is capable of giving. This empowered me to rise up in warrior mode. If I have to go it alone, I'll go it alone, I've done it before and succeeded.

It takes some people one smack to lose their faith and forget their purpose. Jesus endured more than four dozen lashes and he still hung in there through the bruising, the lacerations, the infection, the nerve damage, the excruciating pain, the emotional strain, the tearing and bleeding of the skin. I can take hundreds of lashings and have because warrior souls are built to withstand pain.

Even while being pulled across the dirt with my armor scraping and clinging to my body, and my sword being dragged behind me as I claw towards salvation, I clairaudiently hear my Spirit team through the thud as their force takes over. My clairvoyant vision ahead is of the sky cracking open with Light and the words echoing, "Stand up child."

Crawling out of the Earth plane gasping for air,

strength, and energy, the soul part of me makes it out of the horridly dense Earth plane and at the foot and doorway into the next dimension. I fall to my knees defeated as my physical body gives out and I can no longer be contained in its beaten vessel. Back home we never falter or weaken, but in this Earthly plane the struggle between whom my soul is back home and the human body in this plane causes some contradicting behavior. My forehead lowers touching the ground, which instantly ignites a huge burst of positive strong Divine energy that shakes the ground and lights up slamming around me.

This Light force vibrates with the magnitude of ten destructive Earthquakes overpowering my human physical body and crushing it in the process. Who I really am and not the mask I wear, breaks through and out of my body shooting upwards rapidly at the speed of sound. It looks like a ray of colored light travelling vertically into the sky like a rocket that breaks the clouds apart in an explosion.

This is how the souls move in the heavenly realms. Eyes look away and towards where you want to go next and you're instantly soaring into that place envisioned. The ray of light travels quickly you don't even realize that you were traveling. Meanwhile, my physical human body disintegrates into dust and penetrates the Earthly ground with all traces disappearing.

If you you've seen the front cover of this book, the image was intended to convey a snapshot of my soul on the Other Side in Heaven, which like all souls morphs in and out of how I choose. This is why I especially have a fondness for that image than any of the others. As a Wise One soul through Clairvoyant dreams my guides have repeatedly shown me there is a bow and arrow that appears when I choose to use it. This bow and arrow is not to hunt animals, but is used for good as it's aimed towards its purpose of creating a bigger effect. It evaporates in and out of thin air through the will of my soul's intended thoughts. It's much easier to manifest back home than it is on Earth. On Earth, you can work hard in jobs your whole life struggling rarely able to obtain what you've forever dreamed and desired. In Heaven it transpires in a matter of a seconds the moment you will it to happen. I've talked about some of the realms in the first chapter of my book, *Realm of the Wise One*. I've dropped hints and glimpses of reveal of the spirit worlds throughout my work. Spirit Worlds is plural because the Spirit World is not just one place, but contains numerous vast layers, planes, and dimensions. Because of the unlimited complexity of Heaven there will be psychic glimpses and foresights of the many heavenly worlds that exist through myself and other souls on Earth that have strong psychic visions.

Every soul is made by God, which is why some see Him as their parent, rather than their own parents. Souls reside in different areas, realms, and dimensions in Heaven. They are not all in the same place like they are on Earth. Even though all souls can travel wherever they choose to be. They still like to have one place they call home even on the Other Side, just like on Earth. If a soul is a free spirited soul in Heaven, they may have a place they call their home base, even if they're out and about traveling through all of the infinite vast spaces that exist in Heaven. Souls look to see where they can be of use, since all souls love to be of service in some way. On Earth, you may be trained to serve yourself, but in Heaven we serve others under the Light.

You may have had repeated dreams and visions of where your soul's home is. The dreams and visions would be repetitive throughout your life rather than a fleeting one time vision. This is how most psychic information comes in. It will come in repeatedly to indicate it's authentic. This is pending you're not intoxicated on anything, which will warp what you think you're getting.

There are so many places on the Other Side a soul resides in or moves to. If there are over eight billion souls in a human body on Earth, then they're not all going to head to the same place. Unlike Earth, God and Heaven don't believe in overcrowding or building structures on top of one another or filling the streets with so many people and cars that no one can focus.

Some people will continue to repeat another human life the way you go to another grade in School to continue your education. This is with the hopes that the soul will have that breakthrough into their consciousness that prompts them to evolve out of the limited consciousness they were previously residing in. Regardless of which part you reside in Heaven, all souls are free, courageous, and fearless. They all display joy, love, peace and high-octane upbeat energy always. It's what truly being alive feels like if one could get that way naturally without any toxins or substances.

When things get tough for you on Earth, then you have to snap back into soul reality and look at the bigger picture. This helps you remember that none of it is real in the larger sense. It is easy to become distracted by what seems like something important on Earth, but is just trivial in the end. No one is ever in true harm and it's easy to lose sight of that while living in the epicenter of toxicity. It is merely a tiny experience within a moment in time that will be non-existent a thousand years from now, except besides floating around somewhere in that consciousness of yours.

The Other Side is always recounted by others, including myself as magnificently beautiful, which I know is a vague description. It can be challenging to describe the feelings associated with its magnificence, because no words can do that justice. Some of what exists on the Other Side is nearly identical to Earth's, except that it's shall I say cleaner. There is no wear and tear, erosion from the passage of time, or destruction and harm that human beings would cause on Earth such as violence and vandalism. The natural wonders on Earth also exist in Heaven, but on a grander scale if you can imagine that overbearing and overpowering visual. Some of the wonders that human beings created on Earth also exist in Heaven such as the Pyramids of Giza, the Taj Majal, the monolithic statues, the Petra, the Great Wall of China, or the Teotihuacan, to name a few of them.

One of the reasons it mirrors Heaven is to give the soul familiarity of where it came from. Many of the human built wonders that I listed as examples came from those designer's Divine guidance memories of Heaven, even if they weren't cognizant that this is where the idea is originating from. A great deal of creativity by artists receive similar Divine inspiration without realizing it. One might question why create a replica on Earth if it already exists in Heaven. The complicated reasoning is newborn souls need to be sent to a distant faraway place separate from Heaven to learn and grow. A prestige's place like Heaven knows that if souls were born and left to run rampant creating all sorts of destruction, then they risk being pulled into the Darkness. God would rather create a separate place that is somewhat similar enough to invoke memories of home. This would be the same way you recall your childhood hometown if you're no longer living there.

In Heaven, the weather is sunny, warm, and beautiful around the clock with temperatures that would mirror Earth's but in the 70's. There is no rain or snow, but there are winds that are of the light breezy variety while occasionally speeding up slightly once in awhile. There are a different variety of animals that mirror the animals on Earth, but the animals in the spirit worlds that would be predators on Earth are harmless in Heaven. There are insects, but they only exist in the darker Hell layers of the spirit world that are in different spirit planes entirely. Sorry for those that are insect enthusiasts.

One of the more unbelievable things that exist in the spirit world's are those creatures that people on Earth naively believe to be mythological. These would be things like Unicorns, Mer folks, Fairies, and much more. Those mythological creatures on Earth came from Divine perception. I was never personally a believer in mythological creatures. Never thought much of it until the visions of the different spirit worlds began growing stronger through my Clairvoyance channel over the course of time. This was when I was seeing them in grand epic sweeps. The other things that Spirit were telling me psychically we're coming true and these creatures were coming through that same psychic vision.

Back home on the Other Side in one of the heavenly realms is a sea of lush tropical green plant life blossomed into infinity that would put the rainforest to shame. Surrounding throughout it are magnificent jagged mountain peaks of every variety protruding up high. Many of them contain an infinite number of waterfalls of every size from the small to the massive all cascading down into clear bright pools of shimmering light. A radiant bright violet light with white sparkling bright diamond lights pulsating in and out of it soars across the sky and down to the ground as I dissolve out of it and appear physically whole. My soul marched with each foot creating a purpose that shook the ground moving right into the White Crystalline Cathedrals to make a decision that would be impactful to Him.

I said, "I have to go down there again."

I recall the talk with the council out in a warm paradise outside a Cathedral and Castle looking structure where massive Niagara Fall like waterfalls drop down from the Heavens into a glistening bright white glassy pool below it. I was excited to make the soul journey to Earth again, but also took it extremely seriously the way I take any job seriously while here.

A contract was developed that included numerous lessons, experiences, and soul mates I'd have to endure, since a soul cannot come to Earth without having a contract of challenges. It also illustrated one of the main purposes which was to write numerous spiritual books that will forever be available no matter what century it is. They will be books that can help people, which would simultaneously help improve humanity if everyone on the planet adopts the basic spiritual teachings we do. It doesn't matter if someone reads one of my books and doesn't like it. Those that can benefit from it will have it seep into their consciousness. As my Spirit team has said, "Just because someone doesn't like it doesn't mean they don't need it."

Elements of the best parts of your personality today are elements of your soul back home, but on a lower scale since Earth compresses who you were back home. I knew this would happen before coming here, but I agreed to the trip anyway, because I was doing this for God. Earth is His home and He has guests that He created living on it and causing immeasurable destruction to it, themselves, and each other. There are parents that have kids and a beautiful house. The parents go away for the weekend only to come home to find the house in shambles. To say they would be thrilled to see that would be a lie. This is similar to Earth being God's home and His Children inhabiting it and destroying it. That's why I love that saying to make Earth cool again. There are others out there like me and you know who you are and why you are here. If what we do helps awaken someone for the greater good, then it has done its job.

When the time came to incarnate into an Earthly physical body again, I was sucked into a portal that morphed into a large etheric glowing white holographic tube. My light traveled within it like a shooting star that shot out like a rocket so fast that if you turned your head for a second you missed it. I traveled through that tube feeling my soul and consciousness being crushed in a weight of heavy darkness as the higher-self soul part of me dropped into the unfamiliar foreignness of the lower-self.

Knowing the danger of what I was risking my soul thought, "What am I doing?"

Back home there is no such thing as fear or self doubt, but that was shifting the closer I was to puncturing into this plane. The claws of the Darkness reached in towards me giving life to the warped ego within that expanded underneath the Earth's density. The unaccustomed self-doubt manifested out of the fear that I would lose my connection while on Earth.

"Don't let me lose it, don't let me lose it." I continued to say panicked, "If I lose it, I'm gone. This whole trip will have been pointless."

I remember the tube growing darker before I shot into the human body that was just about formed inside my mother this lifetime. My soul snapped into this unacquainted tiny body and was instantaneously crushed down by the weight of it that created a painful bloody scream like a thousand knives plunging into me. It was like putting on an uncomfortably heavy storm drenched coat.

The second my soul slammed and integrated as one with this physical body, my mother's water broke. After I entered into this Earthly life, the memories grew scattered and suppressed partially cutting in and out of my psychic senses over what I recalled as my soul's agreement, but fading in and out of this consciousness. Every cell was suffocating in this unexplainable horror I never thought imaginable from home. Officially trapped and restricted from the movement I had been used to in Heaven, I realized I've changed my mind and did not want to be back here, but it was too late. God will take you through Hell just to get you back to Heaven.

When your soul travels to the Earth plane to be born, you're traveling through a light tube like tunnel that grows more dark, suffocating, and traumatic as you reach your temporary human body where you exit out of your mother this lifetime into this world. Saying that it's traumatic doesn't do it justice, because it is truly a horrifying experience transitioning to Earth. The distressing remains never end for many people as they function through their Earthly lives with that heavy burden on their soul and not knowing why. When you die you move through another similar tunnel, but that etheric dark tunnel and tube is as wide as a small town, and begins to glow lighter the closer you are to reaching home. Transitioning back to Heaven is the extreme opposite experience compared to travelling to the Earth plane. It is much more awesome, amazing, and exhilarating. You travel away from the Earth plane and closer to the Light where it lifts you back up beyond comprehension. If you survived your human birth, then take comfort that the human death is easier than you can imagine. It's like you fly coach to Earth and then first class to Heaven. You're also traveling with others that are making the trip to and from Earth at any given time. It's almost like the infamously crowded 405 freeway in Southern California!

Every single soul has access to their soul's memories outside of its current human life. It's challenging for many to remember it, since one can barely remember every single shred of their childhood this lifetime, let alone what happened before that. It takes exceptional discipline and a hyper psychic sense to retrieve some of it. Some of what I was shown about my soul's birth into this Earthly life may seem contradictory to what some human beings feel to be true that would be contrary to that. There will always be differing views on certain matters. What I'm shown isn't demanding that this is the way it is. I'm just acting as the translator and relaying what I've been shown through the veil is all.

As the soul is traveling to the Earth plane there is a great deal going on during that process. One of those things is that the soul's energy and consciousness is already merging in with the physical body in preparation for its arrival during the human pregnancy, since like all heavenly beings the soul can be wherever it chooses to. This is why the soul will also start to feel some measure of pain during the traveling phase, because the physical body on the Earth plane experiences pain. The soul that will inhabit that body is simultaneously connecting some of its consciousness into it before the complete soul and physical unification. Meanwhile, the physical body is growing within the human mother at the same time.

When the soul is fully integrated with the physical body, then that's when the physical birth into the Earthly world is about to happen.

If the physical body dies before being born whether through an abortion, miscarriage, or any other complications, then the soul's journey is abruptly halted and it's sucked back through the tunnel to the Other Side. Due to its strengthened psychic senses, it knows what went wrong or what happened. The same goes for if the physical body dies as a baby not long after being born, then the soul is also pulled back home to Heaven. Although, if that soul's human mother ends up having another child, more often than not, the same soul that was intended to merge before the previous complications will usually unite with the physical body of the mother's next pregnancy. This is pending that she gets pregnant again and the child survives, so it's the same soul, but in the newborn child.

All souls suffer quite a bit with much of it suppressed within the memory bank. Every single one of the eight billion souls on Earth at this time have endured the traumatic journey to come here and for some more than once. We can all take in more than can be grasped, which means you're stronger than you may give yourself credit for.

Born into this particular lifetime on March 5, 1973 at 6:28pm in the Los Angeles suburb of Arcadia, California for the astrologers out there. Arcadia is much different today than during the time I was growing up. I moved to the beach in 1990 and have been in beach cities since, except for the short stint in Hollywood. There was a reason I chose to come here at this time in history.

The power, light, and force of God and my Spirit team have always been alive within me vibrating at various degrees depending on my state of my mind.

Finding the right frequency to hear God and your angels requires some effort. Being a Clairsentience psychic sensitive, I pick up on every nuance around me, where I'm acting as a pendulum vacillating from the lower self to the higher self on any given day depending on what energies have been absorbed. This pendulum swings back and forth every minute like the ticking of a clock. When it swings into the space of the higher self, then I'm in the higher frequencies where I hear Heaven our home. When it swings back down in frequency, then a heavy dark foreboding feeling takes over burying my higher self underneath an avalanche of rubble. Like clockwork, I begin to re-align and break through the rubble. As the rubble cracks, Light rips in, and breaks the rubble apart freeing my higher self. This part of my soul soars up into this Light where I hear God again.

This is when the messages and guidance come in clear as if they're standing next to me communicating through my Clairaudience channel. I need to say it or write it down quickly before the pendulum swings back down again into the lower self where I've grown further away from Heaven. Once it drops back down the voices of spirit grow dim or vanish. A developed amnesia rises up where I recall nothing of what I was just told, until I re-break through the rubble asking to be told what was said. The second I break out of the physical plane and back into the Light again, the same messages come in and my memory is restored. This is when I quickly write it down before it's lost. This is also why I cannot be interrupted while in this trance channel, as everything will be lost. It takes steady disciplined effort to hone in with laser sharp focus. I'm a disgruntled soul when I'm yanked out of a channel without my permission.

The good visions are welcomed, but it's the bad ones

75

that can be jarring. I'm affected as if it's happening to me personally. That's a fine line to be walking between this world and the other worlds. I've always given the appearance of being aloof, detached, and sometimes lost somewhere else, because all of this stuff is happening randomly and sporadically every second. It was less comfortable experiencing that as a child and a teenager, because your human emotions at that time are not fully developed to be able to withstand that kind of intensity. As a result, I am a walking intensity. The anxieties I have daily are also connected to these psychic clair senses as well as the childhood abuse. When messages are repeatedly attempting to come through, I may be unknowingly blocking it, which can create anxiety that has no origin. It's a repetitive disruption that for the most part I've learned to not mind it as much.

It's not like I hang out with people and list the spirit encounters going on through each day. It's just another day for me that it isn't worth discussing. It's the same way when I was working jobs before the author career. It's not like I talked about work. I'm at work all day and don't want to talk about it unless there was something important that happened, but most of the time when I was done with work, I wasn't talking about it and instead enjoying life.

This is the same with the psychic spirit circumstances. I don't want to discuss it. I want to enjoy life and kick back and have a good time. If something happens psychically, I brush it off, or I may weave it into a sentence if it's important with someone. When I'm working on a book, then my focus is on the book at that time. When I'm not writing or I take a break, then my mind is elsewhere. I can turn it off to an extent when I walk away from writing. I don't talk about what I'm working on while I'm working on it.

CHAPTER SIX

Personal Stories Of Psychic Phenomena

In the coming chapters we'll focus on a series of mini-psychic and mediumship related examples in my own life. This might offer some illumination into how you can come to psychic information on your own. If anything else, if you enjoy reading stories about psychic phenomena it may be interesting, inspiring, or entertaining.

If I wasn't paying attention to my Spirit team, then I would've run into irreversible catastrophes. There isn't an hour in the day that doesn't go by when I'm not in constant communication with them.

In the psychic worlds, the more something is hidden,

then the stronger the spotlight hits it. Let that be a warning to the cheaters out there. Unsurprisingly, cheating is one of the easier things I see quicker than other things. Part of that is because someone is trying to desperately hide and suppress it. The more you try to hide something, then the clearer it is in the etheric worlds. From a personal view, seeing infidelity is not something enjoyable to see because it causes unnecessary negative feelings that can temporarily cripple someone's life.

The way psychic hits come in may seem pointless. For example, while at a dinner party this guy across from me is talking with me for awhile about deep things.

He asks when my birthday is, I tell him, then he says, "Oh, mine is in August."

I stare him down, "August 5th?"

He lights up smiling from ear to ear, "Yeah! My birthday IS on August 5th. That's pretty good. Wow that's...hmmm. How did you nail it down like that?"

There have been times that people around me might be gabbing away trying to figure an issue out, then one by one they start looking over at me waiting for something to come out of my mouth that will be the answer they're looking for.

In the past, I've made the mistake of accidentally revealing things that are none of my business where I've spoken out of turn. Someone close to me is looking forward to something that's going to be happening in their life and all the plans they're going to do with it. I tactlessly interrupt with casual nonchalance blurting out, "I wouldn't bother doing that, because I thought this was ...."

They've shouted in a panic, "Wait what!? What do you see?"

At that moment I pull back quickly recognizing that

it's not something that has taken place yet. When I'm saying it, then sometimes it feels or seems to me that it's already happened. Once my confusion on it simmers down I then back track to clean up my bluntness. "Never mind. Forget what I said."

They're dead silent knowing it's possibly something important, since they've had enough conversations with me to know the circumstance ends up transpiring the way I thought it already did. The reason I'll sometimes brush it off is because I don't want to crush someone's excitement or dreams unless there is imminent danger. Time passes on and then the friend will eventually come back to tell me the event that I said would or would not take place did that day.

What I was seeing appears to already have happened for them. When in reality it was a forecast Clairvoyant projection that made me believe it already took place.

A situation would happen and friends are all talking over each other about it. One of them would shout, "Well, wait a minute, didn't Kevin say this was going to happen days ago?"

Everyone grows quiet remembering as each pair of eyes turns to look over at me in amazement. When that scenario became a repetitive cycle, another friend I remember chimed in with, "I've learned to just pay attention to whatever you're saying because stuff happens following a statement you've casually mentioned in conversation."

Those closest to me were the first to point out the uncanny predictions that were coming true. Part of that is because I sometimes develop amnesia about what I said unless I write it down or someone has told me that it transpired.

If you're trying to develop your psychic prowess, I

recommend keeping a journal or notepad where you write down anything that comes to you throughout the day, regardless if it seems ridiculous. You can email it to yourself as well and keep it in a folder marked especially for that. Put down the date and what divinely guided psychic information you received. This is one of the better ways to make note of where you're at with your psychic abilities. Because sometimes the psychic stuff that comes in may not transpire for awhile. By the time it does months or even years later, you may not remember that you actually did receive that accurate psychic hit. The only way to recall it is if you wrote it down. You can even go as far as to note the state of mind you were in when your psychic accuracy was on the mark to notice if there is a pattern.

PSYCHIC SENSE OF FOREBODING

Some of the challenges that arise when your psychic gifts are strong is the emotion and anxieties that come with it. There have been nights where I'm yanked awake in strangulation frantically attempting to pry apart a strong heavy force placed on my chest and around my neck. This can indicate a psychic hit that's rolling in on an intenser level. It might be a foresight of a warning, danger, or a catastrophe is near. This hit doesn't necessarily indicate that it's in my personal life, but sometimes it can be. Other times it can be about someone I know or don't know, but that I come across later in the day. There are times that it will be a foreboding sense of the overall Universal energy of the day, such as when the World Trade Center tragedy took place on September 11, 2001. It can also be a dark energy that has infiltrated my barrier and got to me as well too. When this strong dark attack comes in, then the two beings I generally immediately call on that release it are Archangel Michael and Jesus Christ.

Archangel Michael is the main one that dives in during those episodes more than any other since he acts as my own personal security force. He's like a bodyguard nightclub bouncer extricating all danger away from me as much as possible. Some of the times I'm unaware there is danger around me until I see Archangel Michael rising up in front or behind me with his light sword leaned over in front of me to block out what's there. That's when I sometimes realize it's dangerous, "Uh-oh. What?"

It's like a parent standing outside with their hands on their hips glaring at the bad seed friend you're talking to.

Jesus Christ is the other one that frequently shows up for me as well. As a child, I had not understood that I should be calling the Light in. I would just stare at the horrifying sight in front of me that puts me on high alert. This also goes even deeper than what I see, but is also a warning to others that anyone can be infected by the Darkness. No one is immune to the Darkness latching onto them no matter how spiritual you are.

Had I learned to call Archangel Michael and Jesus Christ in as a child, I have no doubt the child abuse would not have been so ongoing. This I pray right now that any child enduring any kind of bullying or abuse, no matter how traumatic, physical, emotional, or psychological, please pray daily and call in God, Archangel Michael, and Jesus Christ as soon as possible. Do this fervently daily without question. In fact, this should still be done even when things are going amazing for you too.

Speaking of Archangel Michael, in another spiritual vortex hot spot on the planet in Ojai, California, I was driving down a pitch black dark winding road on a mountain with no other cars for a half an hour. Lightening flashed like a disco strobe light followed by the pounding of the Thunder. Like a horror film the rain flushed down in a rage pelting the car. It's now midnight and another friend is texting me, "Where are you?"

I spoke back through Siri, "On some mountain somewhere."

It took another ten minutes before it was realized the GPS no longer knew where I was, since it kept directing the car around the same roads in a gigantic circle. When I noticed the same sign on the road appearing for the third time I mumbled, "Oh for heaven sake, this is ridiculous. Archangel Michael!"

Heard his voice clearly through Clairaudience to: "Take the next left and then a quick right. Stay alert or you'll miss it."

Turn-turn, out of the loop, and off and running. Eesh.

It's pitch black in parts of Ojai at night that I went to get something out of my car and ended up walking into the bushes. You could hear my voice ruffling through the darkness, "Oh-COME-on."

Sometimes calling out to God or your Guides for immediate help is all you need to do, then follow their guidance.

REMOTE VIEWING

Remote Viewing is another pretty common psychic related phenomenon in my world. I'm on the phone with a film producer friend of mine whose telling me about another film studio production he's working on. I thought I saw an image flash in front of me causing me to interrupt as I often do as if it's an interview or radio show

I chimed in with what I thought I saw with a question mark, "Absinthe?"

Confused he asks, "What?"

I said, "Absinthe."

Puzzled he asks slowing down his speech, "What? How did you get that? No, I said the Dolly Track had to be reconfigured."

I'm perplexed, "Hmph. Okay. That's odd. I could've sworn I....never mind, sorry go ahead."

He continues on, then stops his story and with excitement shouts, "Oh wait a minute! I'm staring at a bottle of Absinthe sitting on a cart that someone gave me a few days ago. This is unreal. How wha- you mean to tell me you can see this?!" He starts laughing, "This is incredible."

I was quiet and let him have his day about it, as I didn't know why I was seeing that. You can see with that scenario that psychic foresight or remote viewing doesn't always have a profound reason for coming into a soul's psyche. When your psychic antennae is bouncing off the charts, then random things come in that seem to have no rhyme or reason.

On another day I'm on the phone with a female friend of mine. At one point she says something that many women enjoy (and some men), but I could careless about it and they know it. Things like clothes, heels, hair and make-up, etc. Out of nowhere she says she's disappointed in this make-up she got for her face that is falling apart. She officially lost me and in my typical blunt nature rolling off my tongue was, "Oh, your Violet Plum shit."

She gasps and then laughs in excitement, "Yes! That is what it is! Oh my God, this is unbelievable."

I said with my sometimes typical cold distance, "Are you kiddin' me? Is Violet Plum really what's on it?"

She exclaims with excitement, "Yes! I'm telling you that is what it's called. I'm gonna text you a pic of it right now."

I opened the text image and there it was in front of me. A compact make-up thing with the words on it that said: "Violet Plum".

These are minor examples of Remote Viewing. Sometimes it's over useless details and other times significant, all of which are proven or end up being accurate. I have no way to train someone to do it because I'm not trained. It's just a part of me that comes in naturally the same way you breathe. There's no process, tools, or seminars to take. My body and soul are the tool. The more someone cleans up their physical life and gets their feet wet in the spiritual worlds and evolves their soul, then these things can come in easier for them too.

There are numerous remote viewing episodes happening regularly in my life, but I wanted to offer a couple of quick examples. The psychic information came in through various uncontrolled ways. There was no meditation or words said. It came in out of nowhere while I was having regular friend conversations with people.

A psychic hit could be mixed in with clairaudience and then claircognizance in the same breath. In these two particular example cases, the remote viewing came in visually in front of me that it felt like I was physically looking at the items. The first guy was talking for awhile telling me this story and the absinthe bottle was sitting in front of my face with the label on it. It was dominating for reasons unknown to me. I said the word out loud because the force of it was that strong. He and I obviously realized afterwards that he was looking at the bottle in his house where he was sitting. I was unknowingly at the time peering through his eyes at it, which is pretty trippy for some people to comprehend.

With the gal pal, she was droning on about her make-up, which I was totally uninterested in. I could feel my metaphysical eye zooming onto the make-up name. The words were hanging on the tip of my tongue. I could feel it that it rolled off loudly and uncontrollably where I blurted it out not realizing that it was right. I don't know anything about make-up. I didn't even know the color I said existed. As I was blurting it out, I wasn't paying much attention as to why those were the things that came forward. I seem to be ignorant at times as to what is reality in front of my physical eyes and what is coming through the spiritual sight. Sometimes they intertwine for me, which can make life challenging moving about in that constant state.

Both friends were exclaiming excitedly all over the place after those cases happened. With the woman, she cried out with glee, "Your psychic radar is so strong!"

I just said, "Well, apparently in this case it's not like I can give anyone the winning lottery numbers. I'm just seeing useless crap like your make-up container for whatever reason. Totally irrelevant unless you plan to use it as murder weapon."

I wasn't trying to look or peer in, it was just happening on its own while having a casual conversation.

TOO CLOSE TO SEE CLEARLY

A friend in the Aviation industry messaged me: "This Virgin America purchase is getting interesting. Who is going to buy them? Delta, Alaska, or Jet Blue?"

I said, "I don't know anything about that."

He replied, "I've been trying to pull cards about this and it's not clear."

"I don't know what to tell you." I said following a number of seconds of silence then, "No, wait, actually I just heard Alaska."

This was through Clairaudience.

Friend said, "I hope not because I feel like Alaska would just dissolve them to get rid of a competitor."

I said, "Sorry, Alaska is all I hear. Hopefully I'm wrong for your sake."

A week later he messages me, "You were right again. The announcement was made today. Alaska bought Virgin Atlantic for 2.6 billion."

This is an example where if someone is deeply invested in desiring an answer to something, then it becomes more challenging to receive that psychic answer. Whereas myself who is completely emotionally detached and could careless about any of this found that the Divine answer came in naturally without effort. This is another reason that working psychics and mediums read with others like them, since they may not be as objective with their own stuff. Sometimes you can be too close to the answer to see clearly.

Incidentally, he knows I'm not fond of people going to me to ask random questions like that, but this was a rarer case where I uncontrollably blurted out the answer.

TELEPATHIC COMMUNICATION

On another occasion, I was on the phone with my mom who was telling me that my stepfather's cat was not friendly at all. You know, an exciting conversation right? She randomly explained that this cat was always hiding somewhere. I asked her what the cat's name was again and that I'm going to try something. As she continued to talk about this animal, I closed my eyes tuning her out briefly while I telepathically communicated with the cat to walk over to my mother. About a minute or two in, my mom stopped talking and instead started shrieking, "Oh my God! Oh my God! He's coming to me! He's coming over to me!?"

Then to me she cried out, "What did you do?? Did you do something? He's never done that before ever. I need to tell Bill *(her husband)*."

I said, "I connected and communicated with him telepathically and asked him to walk over to you was all."

She took a photo of him sitting next to her, then sent it to me while insisting he has never in the history of them having this unfriendly cat done that. Animals have souls. If they did not have a soul, then this would never have been able to happen since it was a telepathic communication between two souls, even though one was in the body of an animal and the other being my own.

CLAIRCOGNIZANCE MIXED WITH TELEPATHY

Sometimes while I'm watching a film I've never seen before, I may clairaudiently hear the dialogue through my etheric channel before it's said in the movie. A few beats later the character says it on screen. There are times I've inadvertently said the dialogue out loud before it's said on screen, then the character says it. I've had new people in my life look over, "I thought you've never seen this before."

I mumble, "I haven't."

They focus on me with their mouth half open in shock learning the same way longtime friends discovered this about me in the beginning days, before they got used to it.

You may be able to relate to this next mini-example. This is a common Claircognizance hit occurrence that many people have noticed in their own lives. I often know who is calling before I've answered the phone or seen the name on my screen. This is pertaining to calls that I'm not expecting. Taking it further, I'll also psychically know why someone's calling, regardless of who it is and whether or not I was expecting the call. I'll often know what the overall content of an email is going to say before I've opened it. There is no clue to the contents of the email with the subject line or sender. I've especially had regular habits of walking to my phone to answer it only to discover it never rang. As I'm walking away from the phone, then it starts ringing for real and I have to turn back around to get it. I've had others witness this while in the room with me. I've informed friends on occasion to answer their phone while we're out and about.

They tell me, "It's not ringing."

I'm stunned, "Oh."

Then a minute later their phone starts ringing and they've jumped and smiled, "Okay, that was weird!"

When talking with others I have a habit of interrupting people and finishing their sentences as to what they were going to say, to which they pause and confirm it.

I'm sure that can be irritating for some people to have someone already know what they're going to say, and then interrupt and finish the sentence for them. I've never had anyone get angry. They agree that what I said was what they were going to say. This is part of having Claircognizance and using Telepathy. This is a common occurrence in people that may not believe in psychic phenomena. They are still picking up on the hits regardless.

Many couples in relationships that are especially close to one another have admitted they seem to finish one another's sentences. Their souls are so telepathically intertwined while in the relationship connection that they both admit to doing this. It definitely adds to helping the relationship thrive to be so in tune with one another. You're able to also intuit what your partner is going through, their needs, and vice versa. This is also an example of a strong soul mate soul connection.

Someone may be telling me something I already know, but it doesn't mean I don't mind hearing it come from them the same way God, the angels, and your Spirit team knows what someone is going to say next. They will still listen as if it's the first time they're hearing it.

CLAIRVOYANT PSYCHIC FORESIGHT

One afternoon, I was at the end of working out on the beach when I slowed down to stroll on the sand along the shore and absorb that glorious uplifting Divine energy in. God and Spirit are exceptionally felt while in a vast nature setting with little to no people. It was a quiet hot day and no one seemed to be around. Out of nowhere, through my Third Eye Clairvoyance psychic sense channel, a bright flash shot up and exploded in front of me. The flash light layers peeled away and this image of a blonde surfer guy was approaching me and asked me if I had the time. I thought that was a totally pointless and irrelevant vision, but it came in super strong enough for it to dominate.

I'm continuing to stroll along the shore as my consciousness is pulling in and out of a trance like state, which is not unusual for me in general especially while in nature. I felt the presence of someone coming up behind me, then I heard a male voice calling out as if he had been calling to me for awhile.

"Excuse me." The voice said.

I whipped around inhaling in shock for a second as if seeing a ghost. This blonde surfer guy holding his surfboard was smiling.

"Do you know what time it is?" He asked.

"Um-yeah, it's..." I'm pulling out my phone and telling him while stunned as it was the same person I just saw in the vision. His smile gradually relaxed refusing to leave studying me as if coming to the realization of something. The start of a longer conversation was kicked off. It grew to where we both recognized that this is a mutual new friend. This is someone I am still friends with today.

You'll note from some of the mini-illustrations in this chapter how sometimes the etheric information coming in is just tiny little random psychic hits that come in out of nowhere. Sometimes the psychic hits are meaningless, yet accurate, and other times they seem meaningless, but end up revealing something bigger taking place like a new friendship, lover, job, home, pet, and on and on.

The way I saw this new friend approaching me now reminds me of the *Hereafter* film I mentioned earlier in the book. There was a scene when the Matt Damon character received a psychic flash of meeting this woman at a café that becomes a romantic mate. The flash takes place through his Third Eye as he smiles, then minutes later he sees the woman in the distance looking around until her eyes land on him. They both smile and approach each other before sitting at one of the café tables.

These examples of psychic foresight were barely a pebble compared to the hundreds of random little psychic hits that have gone on throughout each day for as long as I can remember. Sometimes it's insignificant and other times it leads to something bigger. This is another of the many reasons others have mentioned that I sometimes appear distracted. I'm paying attention to more information than one can handle from both the physical and spiritual worlds. I would never recommend being in my head. You'd end up traumatized and reaching for a drink. The ways my psychic hits come in are often random. It's in the detail that people notice. That detail can be just one word that there is no way you could have possibly have known it. There is nothing I'm doing to make it happen. I'm not conducting a meditation session or any special exercise. I'm just going about my day like it's any other day, but these hits are always coming in on their own. Therefore, I resent anyone that sees psychic work as demonic, because I'm not a working or practicing psychic. It comes in all on its own. It's how the soul was built. When your soul is in tune, then the psychic communication grows stronger by itself as a result of that. There's nothing special about me, because everyone has that capability.

Stay Centered Emotionally

To Access Psychic Information

When you are living as one with the Light, you are empowered, focused, and safe. You are able to grasp the reality that everything is destined to take place in the way the energy is directed and the way it is intended, regardless if you agree with it or not. This is what helps in making accurate psychic predictions.

I've predicted every Presidential election to date in my lifetime, including the most controversial one where Donald Trump was elected President in 2016. I still get asked how I did that as well as praised for never folding on it no matter how displeased people were with that. The reasons are a bit complicated. I never get involved in all of the election talk, while the rest of the world is spending almost two years leading up to it and then some complaining about it daily. There isn't one political post from me unless it's related to Divine Guidance, but even then it's rare.

The reason I bothered to announce the Presidential predictions is to save people time. When you know what's coming up, then you don't waste years of your life whining and gossiping about it daily on social media with friends and family, which is a toxic way to live. It's a waste of time to devote senseless complaints about things that are out of your control, unless you're working with Congress to enact the positive change you seek. Imagine what productive and amazing things could've been accomplished during that time.

I posted a column fifteen months before that election that the runner ups would be down to Hillary Clinton and Donald Trump with Trump being sworn in as

President. This was super early on when the publics interests were with Bernie Sanders and Jeb Bush more than anyone else. No one believed what I said initially including the ones that wanted either of them to win.

Nearly a year after that column, the runner ups were announced in the media that it was down to Clinton and Trump. Following that announcement, my in-box was flooded with mail from people that had seen the earlier prediction. They realized that 50% of my prediction had already come true, which means if I was accurate that early on, then the possibility of me being 100% accurate could be possible.

The darkness of ego continued to be predictable causing endless arguments, noise, dividing, attacking, and violence over it for years. No one wanted to believe it all the way up until he was actually announced as President in the media. I didn't watch the election, but friends did contact me that night to tell me what happened. It was Clinton until the final minute on election night, so it was believed that perhaps the rest of my prediction will not come true. Historically, we know that it did come true when it was announced that Trump won.

I have no emotional interest in human gossip and drama. It is almost impossible to accurately psychically predict something surrounding an area that you have a deep emotional interest in. Your psychic vision is blocked or clouded at that point. This is why the so many on the mark psychics were unable to predict his win. In fact, most working psychics insisted it was Hillary Clinton with others saying it would be Jeb Bush. Many of them ended up taking down those prediction posts, columns, and blogs when it turned out to be untrue.

The reason they didn't get it right was because they

had too much emotional interest invested in who would win. Their original posts on it were bathed in venomous emotional interest instead of remaining emotionally detached for a prediction like that. They might have hated the possible outcome with a malice or spite. That alone is going to psychically block spirit communication. You have to be centered to get or give an accurate psychic reading for yourself or anyone else. It's nearly impossible to psychically read accurately if you have any negative emotion or an emotional investment in the answer. This clouds the psychic foresight because negative feelings block or dim the communication line. This is another reason I've recommended that people get clear minded and focused.

Practice emotional detachment to events so that you can accurately receive any measure of Divine wisdom. If you're not in that state, then wait until you are to conduct a reading with your Spirit team.

In general, I tend to view things from the perspective of God and my Spirit team. When you've been around working with them for as long as I have, and they've always been on the mark having proved that to me time and time again, then I stick with them and trust in them rather than anything or anyone else.

As for how the psychic prediction with this came about, I had Clairvoyantly seen it come down to Clinton and Trump. Their names flashed in front of me immediately after I asked who would the nominees be. When I then asked who would the next President be, my guides kept showing me a Clairvoyant image of Donald Trump's hand over a Bible that was running like a mini-video clip on repeat. This same vision never stopped even when those that opposed him insisted it would never be him. I would continuously be asked, "Are you sure it's still him?"

I grabbed a deck to quadruple check, which is what I do when I need additional insurance. They gave me the Knight of Wands card, which to me shows someone winning, so the answer was yes I'm sure.

The results were always the same no matter how many times I checked. I would tell people when asked, "It will be him. It's all I psychically see. I've repeatedly checked. The answer doesn't change."

The moral of this story? If you are attempting to get information psychically, you cannot have any measure of an emotional attachment to the outcome. You need to take the higher view of God and the angels, which is always neutral and objective. No negativity or judgment of any kind can be in your heart and soul. In general, my personality disposition is an emotionally detached one anyway. Part of having been raised in a harsh abusive environment ended up offering a positive benefit with the strong composure bit. There can be some positives gained even from the most atrocious of circumstances. In this case, I was given a tool that could be applied to other areas of my life from the personal to career and work life.

As one former boss once told others about me, "People can be upset about something and not handling anything well, but Kevin is always unruffled by any of the drama going on."

Another said, "You're the calm inside the storm."

Emotional detachment can serve you well in the end and save quite a bit of wasted time. While the masses continued to waste years posting their political complaints and rants that did nothing to change anything, God and my Spirit team had me continue to work for them. I ignored the noise of the public and ended up writing seven additional Divinely guided books during that time. Are you going to waste years seeking out negative toxic time wasters or will you get to work on your soul's purpose and contribute to making a beautiful life happen?

PSYCHIC MESSAGES TRANSMITTED VIA

CLAIRAUDIENCE AND TELEPATHY

To protect this person's anonymity in the following psychic phenomena example, I'm using the word 'ex' as their name. One of my exes moved out of the state and ended up in a relationship with someone else. We were officially over after being on and off for twelve years, and no further contact or communication was made during that time. A year had gone by and I had gone on working hard to forget all about this person when suddenly my exes name continued to fly through my Clairaudience channel. It sounds like a name entering your mind may be no big deal, but the way it comes in psychically is accompanied by an intense Clairsentience feeling weight on my chest, so I knew it was important.

This continued repeatedly day after day for six weeks straight attacking my psyche. Within the middle of that time period, my ex randomly showed up in a Clairvoyant dream, which hadn't happened in years. I called friends to tell them all of this was happening out of nowhere and won't stop. My guides were insistent on saying my exes name repeatedly that it was driving me into insanity, because of how intense it was. I had no inclination or interest in communicating with this ex, I did not miss this ex, I was done, and moved on. It took a great deal of work and time to get to that space. There was a strong enough emotional detachment to the ex that I knew it was a psychic hit about something pertaining to this person. I then screamed to my Spirit team with both hands clawed over my head as the repetitive psychic hit was causing my physical body pain. "Get my exes name out of my head!! Why are you putting it in there?!"

It quieted down for the night, but then the next day it started back up more persistently. I stood up arms outstretched and completely centered back in warrior mode calling in my entire team. "Get it out and banish it out of me now! In all directions of time this is over. Remove my exes name from my consciousness. I am not interested."

And just like that it stopped and was followed by an eerie silence taking over. I was relieved that those psychic episodes were gone after weeks of this repeatedly slamming into my senses. However, by me banishing the name out with such severity, this triggered the ex to then send me a random email message through a social media account. The message said, "Well I sent a message on your birthday about a month ago, but you hadn't read it."

That was it. Nothing else. I stared at the message and thought, "That's strange. I don't remember seeing anything."

My birthday was six to seven weeks prior, so apparently this message was sitting there that whole time without me seeing it. Obviously, this seemed to be a big enough deal for this ex whose thoughts were being plagued wondering what's happened with me. This is because I'm typically responsive, but this time not only had it been over a year of no communication, but I also haven't replied or read this exes email sent six to seven weeks prior. The intensity of that feeling the ex was experiencing over it was strong enough for a prolonged period that it triggered the Clairaudience psychic hit I was receiving during that time attempting to get my attention.

This is an example of numerous things going on here related to psychic phenomena. One of them is that I was receiving this severe psychic hit of the name Clairaudiently being slammed into my head repeatedly in such an intense Clairsentience way that it was causing me physical pain. The weight of it was a force to be reckoned with. I Claircognizantly knew it was a message, but my ego wasn't interested in that message. When I say that the name was coming in repeatedly, this isn't where it's said then it goes away, then comes back later. No, it was an etheric voice repeating the exes name like a broken record. When I'd ignore it, it would come in louder and repeated like this, "Ex, ex, ex, ex, ex, ex, ex, ex." It would happen, and then again an hour later, and so forth throughout each day. My hands clawed on top of my head with despair and frustration for weeks, "Please stop. I don't want to know why this is coming in."

This is also an example of telepathic communication between two souls. This exes' thoughts and feelings were potent enough that it was reaching me through my guides. Many deep soul connections between two souls are in constant telepathic communication. This is regardless if the person is a friend, lover, ex-lover, or family member. It can also be a communication with one soul on Earth and another in Heaven, and with those that are no longer in your life such as in my situation.

Telepathic communication is one of the primary ways of communicating in Heaven. There is no effort in that way of communication in the Spirit Worlds. This ability is part of the whole gamut of psychic clair senses that exists within your soul in the human body. You can transmit thoughts and feelings to someone through telepathy. This is just one tiny example where it was going on in my world without me wanting it or doing it. This other soul was able to transmit that communication to me through my guides hoping I'd act on it and investigate further. My ego did not want to act on it as the relationship had been a long running complicated one and I worked hard to move on. I didn't want to pursue it further to discover why the name was constantly coming in. As soon as I demanded my guides remove it in such a powerful way that it went dead quiet around me, that was when it triggered a psychic alert and transmitted this information to this exes Clairsentience channel causing a breaking point to take place. This pushed the ex to locate me and send me that message.

This is one illustration amidst countless telepathic communication hits taking place in my day to day life. This psychic scenario seems miniscule, but we're living an Earthly practical life on top of the soul experiences, lessons, and growth work. When you notice these little psychic hits in your day to day life, then it can be relaying messages that your Spirit team is wanting to tell you, even if you don't want to know about it the way I didn't initially. I let that go once I realized this person missed me so intently that it was powerful enough to reach me clairaudiently and telepathically.

CHAPTER SEVEN

Wonders Of Mediumship

Psychic and mediumship phenomena has been around for centuries dating on back to the dawn of humankind. In ancient Egypt and during the Christ days, prophecies were foretold by wise ones that people noticed were later coming true. The interest in the phenomena has only continued to grow since. Eventually superstition and disbelief among those that didn't understand what psychic communication truly is began to push back against this rising phenomenon. This was followed by a period in history when anyone that could be considered a psychic would be killed. This means you'd be a target even if you weren't interested in psychic pursuits, but displayed behavior that was considered unusual to the robotic trained ways of the rest of society.

Superstition and disbelief has always ran through the minds of the limited. Hyper religious extremists felt that it was demons, darkness, and evil taking over that psychic person, or the person was succumbing to Devil worshipping. There are Devil worshippers around the world, but that shouldn't be confused with psychic phenomena or mediumship. The detractors may have a small point as far as conjuring up a malefic dark spirit that could pretend to be good. There are people that still believe that superstition, but the difference today is they have no authority over anyone that partakes in psychic practices. They can no longer behead you, burn you at the stake, or boil you to death.

In the late 1800's and into the 20th Century, Edgar Cayce was one of the popular psychic authors who had a more scientific and metaphysical approach to psychic phenomena, which made it more receptive to scholars who were less inclined to read something they felt to be a bit on the woo-woo side as some say. This doesn't mean he wasn't without criticism and detractors, since those will always exist by those that don't understand something firsthand.

There was a time during the 1960's when a hopeful peace and love movement rose to prominence. People were also experimenting with drugs more than they ever had. This led to hallucinations that confused the person into believing they were having a spiritual experience. When I was a drug addict and alcoholic in my early twenties, my psychic connection was dimmed down to the point it was difficult to pick up on anything. It was that master life class I dove into that told me your psychic connection is blocked while under any toxic influence.

This is part of the reason quite a bit of crimes happen when you're under the influence. You are not able to detect psychic warnings from Spirit that you're headed towards an unsafe circumstance with someone that is no good or that a dangerous person will be entering the bar, club, or music venue. This is also why those establishments have historically been easy targets for shooters, because no one is in a clear mind to pick up on Divine warnings.

This isn't telling anyone to not go to a bar or similar venue. It's illustrating why drugs and alcohol prevents or blocks one from connecting with the Divine. It can open the gateway to malefic spirits, because like evil people they know you're easily accessible in that state for anything and anyone. This is being said as I learned the hard way having been through that experience myself.

As human life progressed, this also gave way to another growing interest in the psychic phenomena world, which is Tarot card reading. The Tarot started to rise up in popularity around the 13th and 14th Century. This popularity has never waned, which has turned off religious extremists that believe you are on your way to Hell if you practice. Unpredictably, this also gave rise to the naysayers, skeptics, and critics, but they will always exist even if you sit still and do nothing.

The Tarot is a great way to receive answers from God and your Spirit team during those moments you're blocked. Ultimately, your soul is a psychic vessel and Divination tools are not necessarily needed. The dangers of the Tarot or using Divination tools is that you could be communicating with a dangerous spirit, but that can happen regardless if you use Divination tools, you're an extreme religious person, or atheist. Everyone is susceptible to dark spirits, which is evident if you take a look around at how bad human behavior dominates the planet. Tarot is the least of the critics worries. At least with experienced Tarot readers they are taking it seriously and conducting safe psychic practice while only inviting in the highest vibrational spirits. It's the inexperienced readers that should be cautious and ensure they use soul protection.

Decades following the 1960's someone could still be branded a hippy if they had an Earthy spiritual vibe, as if that's a negative thing. By the time the United States moved into the 1970's and 1980's, they saw another growing interest that included psychic mediums writing best selling books like Sylvia Browne, who was one of the more popular ones then. Many psychics and mediums of that time began to use the marketing plug that they are world renowned and have special psychic gifts that God gave them. They are good at their job and what they do in the realms of psychic phenomena, but they are inaccurate about the special gifts given only to them. Every soul on the planet is born with their own set of special psychic gifts, but most are unaware of it unless they develop or pay more attention to it. Some of those gifts may vary from one person to the next. The more intuitive someone is, then the stronger their psychic gifts may be. All souls have that capability when they practice and connect often.

Once the technological age came about and social media took over after the year 2010, more people were discovering their spiritual gifts on their own. They realized there is more to this life than the physical superficial mundane. It is making it easier for them to express these talents on the world wide web. It is also giving more people access to spiritual related information by being guided to the right teachers, motivational speakers, holy ones, and priests.

As with anything, the dangers with that is what's posted on the Internet or social media is often taken as fact. A popular social media person might post a blog or spiritual content that is inaccurate, then other followers will take that and re-hash and re-post it. Suddenly people are copying and pasting the same information over and over believing it and not realizing it's not accurate. I've had readers point out they've seen this with the whole Soul Mate and Twin Flame movement stuff specifically. This is where the meanings of Twin Flames got so twisted up with the rise of the Internet use that it's no longer accurate. It reminded me of how the media acts today. They'll pick up a story from another news source and recycle it, then the masses believe it because it's coming from a popular influencer. Years later it's finally discovered to be inaccurate, but no one notices or cares, because they've moved onto other things.

The dangers of anything online is that false information gets thrown around and picked up like wildfire. You have this mighty movement of inaccuracies being spread. Just because someone has a million followers doesn't necessarily mean they are posting accuracies. They were just able to master the art of social media followers online. You take that illusion away and there isn't much left. There was a day that Instagram and Facebook had shut down for most of the day due to a major technical problem during the Mercury Retrograde no less. It wasn't long after it was re-instated when people were putting some pretty funny memes up.

They said things like, "Instagram shuts down leaving 56 million smart phone selfie models and 183 million critics unemployed."

Others posted memes that said, "Instagram needs to

shutdown for a year so people can go back to being themselves."

The most factual teacher may not have a social media account or they have a smaller following because they're not interested in playing the social media game of attracting in likes and followers. That person might be that Native American Wise One in his eighties that lives out in vast areas of nature free of technology, rather than logging online to post randomness and inaccuracies on social media.

Mediumship and Psychic are two completely separate abilities. Mediumship is the ability to communicate with those that have crossed over to the Other Side. I've been informed by many that have had mediumship readings where they said the medium is on the mark with the information being relayed from the deceased loved one that it's uncanny. Those same people have gone back to the medium for a psychic reading about other things and found that the medium was off or inaccurate. Nothing they predicted came to pass.

The reason is the reader is a medium, but not a psychic. They are more accurate when connecting with a loved one that passed on, but not necessarily with the psychic prediction stuff. It also doesn't mean they have no psychic abilities, since everyone does, but it just means their mediumship abilities dominate. Go to a medium to connect with a loved one that passed on and have information relayed by them. Go to a Psychic if you want a future prediction reading.

Psychic readings are probable forecasts that relay the current life trajectory pattern if things continue as they are. This can change depending on free will choice by all parties. There are also some people that have both strong mediumship skills and psychic abilities. Every soul has these gifts built deep into the pilot light of their soul. Many don't know that or have not developed it. You wouldn't know it if you are living an Earthly existence that is on the surface, shallow, and superficial side.

An excellent psychic will typically be about 70-80% accurate on average. This is also why it's been seen that some Psychics and Mediums have been wrong. I remember there was enormous backlash on Sylvia Browne for getting some critical things wrong, but what her detractors ignored were the many critical things she's got right. There is that myth or debate that if someone is psychic then they must know all. This criticism comes from those that don't know anything about psychic phenomena. The irony is those same people have psychic abilities within them too, but they're blocked unable to pick up on anything except what's coming from their ego that primarily drives them.

I'm sure you've heard this one before, "If she's psychic then why can't she see the lottery numbers."

As if strong psychic abilities are granted for personal financial gain. If that were the case, then everyone would be rich. God and Spirit relay information on a need to know basis, rather than what will help you obtain through greedy means. They do not always reveal psychic information unless it's the right time.

The same way that all souls have some measure of psychic abilities built within them, they also all have mediumship abilities built into them too. They just might not be aware of it is all.

When one plans to receive a mediumship reading, especially those that don't receive psychic or mediumship readings often, their loved ones in Heaven answer that call like a Fireman answering a fire bell. They see that as an opportunity to relay messages to this Medium they've been trying to relay to the person forever, but seem to only be able to do it through an efficient and gifted psychic medium. They will push the person on Earth that is vacillating about whether or not to obtain a reading to do it. The person will later recount how amazing the reader was and knew things that only their deceased loved one knows. Their loved ones that wanted to communicate knew they could get the information across through the gifted Psychic or Medium.

The difference between a skilled Psychic Medium and any other Psychic is the extraordinary one is an experienced professional that is genuinely able to connect with the Other Side. The latter might be someone that is using guess work, or worse they know they're wrong, but don't care as they're making money, which is what gives the psychic a bad name by those that don't understand the phenomena. The unfortunate bit is the ones using guess work or doing it for greed reasons can develop their psychic senses so that they can give accurate readings. If you're already giving readings, then why not work to improve on it?

Growing up I never thought, "I'm a Psychic" or "I'm a Medium". I was displaying those abilities early on, but never used the labels since Heaven doesn't think much about the labels either. I didn't train or learn about any of this through video channels, seminars, classes, etc. There was no Internet when I was a teenager growing up. The spiritual movement hadn't risen to the level it became post technology days in the 2000's and beyond. The spiritual classes I received were coming directly from God and my guides during childhood and the teenage years.

Offering readings was never anything I wanted to pursue or was interested in either. What I was interested in was helping people learn to make sounder choices in life, love more often, live more peacefully, joyfully, and obtain their goals. I knew that if they were connecting to a higher power themselves that it could positively help them reach those things, while also knowing there was more to life than the physical mundane trained early on.

I was a kid growing up in a suburb of Southern California riding my bike or skateboard around town while communicating with the Other Side. I didn't hop on my skateboard and go, "Oh, let me try to connect with Spirit."

They were coming through automatically and I conversed with them. In a strange sense kind of like that little girl in *Poltergeist*, although she was talking to malefic spirits stuck in purgatory, which you never want to do. She was a five year old, so I'll cut her some slack, and it was a fictionalized thriller film. Some of the stuff was close to how it is and the other stuff was made up for entertainment. One of the things that was true in the film was that the spirits stuck in purgatory haunting this home were not aware they had passed away. They just drifted around in a meaningless existence between the Earth and Heaven plane fearful of going into the Light. The stuff that was made up was obviously the special effects light show that it grew to become in the latter part of the film.

I may hear from those that have passed on from this life generally upon death repeatedly on up to about a year. It gradually decreases unless I attempt to spiritually and psychically connect with them for anything. This is because they are moving deeper into the next world and getting to work on their own stuff. They are busy on the Other Side in the way that we are busy on Earth. They are not sitting around bored or waiting for some invisible phone to ring. They will know when someone is missing them because the person missing them on Earth will unknowingly alert them through their senses such as through their thoughts and feelings.

When you think of a loved one that passed on, they are cognizant of it. This is one of the many ways that the deceased are alerted and will then rush to that person's side. They'll offer comfort through the many ways that spirit communicates with you through your psychic clair senses. If you are angry with them, then they will work to produce healing between the both of you. They have a higher perspective after death that is similar to the angels and they want to make amends with you.

Sometimes you may think of them and are unaware that they were sending you a message telepathically that put them into your mind. This is during those moments where all is well and you've been fine since their passing. You're going through the motions in life, then you suddenly think of them randomly out of nowhere. This random thought would be them sending you a message. It could just be a hey, hello, hope all is well message. They might be trying to deliver a more complicated message or to get your attention about something that's coming up in your life to notice.

There are times I could be talking to a friend or someone that lost someone close to them, and while we're talking about other things the person that passed on for them communicates random things to me. They suddenly start to use me to get information across to that person, since they somehow find it easier to access me than the person directly. They were usually trying to access the other person for awhile, but the other person was ignoring it or not as in tune during those moments.

This is another reason my Spirit team and I have offered tips to get others more aligned and in tune in our works. This is so that you can be a full-fledged soul that uses your own psychic senses to get this information on your own. Every soul on the planet is capable of communicating with God and their Spirit team through their psychic clair senses built into their soul. Let them learn how to do it themselves the same way you had to learn to read and write. This is also why spiritual concepts should be taught in grade school. It would make everyone's lives less stressful if the whole planet was on board. It would be nice that after centuries of human evolution that this would've been the case by now.

I had my first reading with someone else when I was eighteen with a friend of mine out of curiosity. It felt like I was sitting with someone like me who could do what I could do. There was a kindred connection through the reading. I appreciate the psychic craft and have numerous friends in the mediumship and psychic practice. These are people I met through my work or they conducted a reading for me. We ended up hitting it off after the reading and becoming friends. Sometimes the readings I've had in the past were for entertainment, while other times I'm guided to by my own team to discover a confirmation. For instance, there was an incident where my Spirit team had me circle the date December 5th as an important date to note. I jotted it down and moved on. Weeks later I had a Medium read me and at one point she said, "By the way, December 5th is an important date for you, but I'm not sure why."

I've had exceptional readers meet me and immediately say things like, "Wait a minute, you're actually a Medium." Or, "You're a writer." When they've said those statements at the top of the read, I can already tell this reader is well connected to be able to see that upon the first thirty seconds.

That was a double confirmation telling me to keep an eye out on that significant date, especially if someone I didn't know pointed it out as well too. Guides will often keep pointing things out including through other people. This way they can hammer home that the information or message is especially important.

The people I know personally that pass on tend to communicate with me not long afterwards. Some of them have come forward in my life to relay or say something to me from the Other Side. Sometimes they might try to help with certain issues or advise on certain things I might be dealing with personally at that time. It's usually volunteered information from them. I take what they're saying with a grain of salt as I would any friend giving me advice on Earth. The advice I follow first comes from God and my Spirit team council over people, including those that passed on. I take it into account, listen to them, and appreciate it as I would any friend on any plane, but it doesn't mean I will or will not follow it necessarily. My friends and I have always had a pact that if one of us passes on that we'll likely be communicating with each other through the veil, since the communication seems to be more direct in that way.

OMINOUS SPIRITS

Since childhood I've been pulled into two different directions that include this plane and some of the others beyond this one. Moving into the other planes is like moving through water where my hand pushes into it effortlessly until it's covered in it.

One of the other many different psychic experiences I recall sifting back into time was when I had gone through my fathers house after his death. The house was officially empty as it was set to be closed up. There was no one living in that house or so I thought. There was no one "living" is the right word were looking for here.

The second my foot stepped into the house I could feel the energy around me. The impressions of spirit received was so abnormally heavy and dark. It wasn't like that during the months after his death while the home still had some people in it. Nor was it like that the other few times I had been in it after it was vacant. It was only after time had passed when I went in that it seemed some unexpected spirits had moved in there freely without paying any rent.

To try to convey what was happening it felt like a thick dark matter enveloped me into suffocation in my chest, while I'm trying to walk through quicksand or mud. Each step I took was pulling my whole spirit and body into the floor. I started to feel a panic rise within me because I was deep within that energy. My heart began to race, breathe accelerated, and worry set it in that I'd have a full blown panic attack because everything was increasing too abruptly fast. I stopped and leaned my hand against the wall as if I was losing my balance. I said to my own Spirit team while breathing between my words, "Please. I. We. I need to get out of here."

There were a number of dark spirits in there. It was a mixture of deep sadness in some of them and so much hate in the others like this heavy oppression.

There are spirits that do get trapped in the Earth plane unknowingly. I wouldn't wish that Hell on my worst enemy. I knew I needed to be cleared immediately afterwards as it had created tiny incision cuts on my light and latched onto me. While outside I called in Jesus Christ and Archangel Michael to baptize me with white light to bring my weakened soul's strength back up, since it had been crushed by the somber energies. I then asked them to help usher those stuck souls into the Light.

STAY CENTERED PSYCHIC WARRIOR

DECEASED LOVED ONE VISITATION

After my father's passing, he mostly came in to help my brother and sisters, especially the youngest sister because she was fifteen when he passed on, which is super young to lose a parent you're close to. They were closer more than anyone else in the family dynamic. This is also because he raised the youngest in a different way. He wasn't abusive in the way he had been with me. This might have something to do with as my mother put it that he's older and not as strong health wise. He also came in to help his ex-girlfriend of seventeen years whom he had the child with. This was all mostly within the first year to two years to help her continue on, as well as to help raise the daughter from the Other Side. He eventually helped guide her to a new love partner years later whom she later married. Many spouses or lovers that passed on will typically be responsible in helping the one on Earth come into contact with a new soul mate, because they don't want them spending the remainder of their Earthly life grieving for them that whole time. They know they'll see them again, and they need them to strengthen from the grieving process to continue on in order to finish their Earthly class.

My father's assistance then waned once the girlfriend had the new mate. He also had other things to do on the Other Side. Anyone that was left grieving ferociously the first year saw an improvement the second year. They were moving on with their lives to one degree. This didn't mean they were forgetting all about him, since they still celebrate the anniversaries of his birthday, death, and holidays, but any pain of missing him was declining. This is what the deceased soul wants to see happen, because they have things to do where they are.

When the one on Earth is grieving for a prolonged period of time, then this pulls them in to try and console and heal them to move on. This moving on doesn't mean you don't care, but they know you have work to do as well.

When you've gained your life back and are continuing on after the loved one passed, then the deceased soul won't hang around as much, because you're doing fine. This is what they wanted. They want you to be fine and to know they are fine. Once we're all fine, then everyone can get back to work in whatever plane they're on. Some of them will routinely check on you, so don't be surprised as the years go by and positive things are suddenly happening for you or you're getting messages that you know is most definitely them. It is!

My father never really came in much around me except to say hey. My team said there were two reasons for that. One was I initially forbade it immediately after his passing since I had been released by his death and had quickly got to work on my main life purpose. Even after I lifted that ban nine months after his death, they said that I didn't need any help. It was other family members that were suffering, but that I was fine and doing great without any help from anybody, so he didn't need to be around as much.

There is one area I always seem to grieve and that's when my serious relationships end. If a serious relationship ended due to my love partner passing on, then I likely would not grieve in that way, because my mindset with that is that it's God's doing. Whereas a general serious relationship ends because they cheated, got tired of the relationship, or left me, then that's a different kind of grieving. What makes that grieving witnessed ironic is that I don't get sad or grieve over much else. I'm moved with emotion by certain circumstances, seeing someone happy, words, art, movies, and music, but being moved is not grieving or sadness. It's being touched by the intensity and depth the particular soul conveys through those art forms.

With my own father's passing in 2010, it's been one death after another around me since. That's when I knew that I've officially been around here for quite awhile! It's when I see everyone around me pass on throughout my life. I see death as a bright new beginning for that soul. I know they have just been released into a spiritual heavenly Disneyland. If they are someone I was close to, then I also know I will see them when I'm done here. And more often than not, especially if it's someone I know, they tend to appear for me right away anyway as illustrated next.

TALKING THROUGH THE VEIL

As I'm driving along the coast one day, my grandmother who I knew was still alive was talking to me through my Clairaudience channel. I was communicating back for about a minute while I drove around the winding curve, then I inhaled sharply in shock. I thought, "Wait a minute. How is this happening?"

This is because the way she was communicating to me was the same way that spirit communicates to me from the Other Side, so it had thrown me off because I didn't know she passed on since she was living in another country at the time.

I quickly starting making calls to various family members leaving messages like, "Where is she? Did she pass on? What's happening? Because she was communicating with me in a way that can only be done from the spirit world. If she's alive, then that's impossible. Maybe she's unconscious. Can someone check on her please."

No one seemed to know, but they grew panicked when I contacted them because they know what I do. They knew I wouldn't be calling if there wasn't something I picked up on that happened.

Turned out my grandmother was staying with one of her four sons. They had brought her into surgery for a health issue. She passed away during the surgery. My Uncle had delayed telling everyone because he hadn't mentioned she was going into surgery to begin with. Having to explain the whole story for some reason was overwhelming to him. Other family members were telling each other that you can't think Kevin won't know or won't find out about something like this.

Everyone around was naturally upset that no one was told that day. There was a bit of drama surrounding that, but I wasn't personally affected by not being told. I understand why he didn't. Part of evolving your soul is you understand things that would normally propel you to drama. You are less likely to overreact to things as you evolve. You take a minute to absorb someone else's truth regardless if you agree of what they did.

MEDIUMSHIP DANGERS

I received a call from a sibling that her friend's nephew committed suicide. The nephew was only sixteen and it left his Aunt in a mournful state. I made an exception to conduct a mediumship session due to this being a young person that took his life. I ended up getting pulled in too deep connecting with him that it stayed long after I came out of the session. I got too far into the other world with him too soon after the suicide that his soul latched onto me without me realizing it right away.

There was a heavy darkness that seemed to pull me under as I came out of the session, but I brushed it off. Moving on with my night all seemed okay, but then hours later it started to feel like I was being physically strangled. It propelled me to get up realizing I was having trouble breathing. My hand glided its way around my throat area because I could feel some pressure. This propelled me into a panic attack as I used my hands to shuffle oxygen into my body. When you feel as if you're being strangled there is no time to consider what's going on. This went on for awhile, but then seemed to lighten up slightly, even though something wasn't feeling entirely right. It was cutting in and out sporadically over a period of time. I thought, "I may need to go see a Doctor tomorrow just to check. Maybe this will be gone in the morning."

I will typically rule out other possibilities before automatically considering there is paranormal activity going on just because someone says there is. There are cases where someone believes that their house is haunted and calls a Medium for help. If a Medium is a strict professional and decides to consider a case, they will go over to the house with skepticism. They rarely ever automatically assume there is a paranormal situation going on in the house. Their job is to first rule out other factors going on in the house from the pipes to a bad light and so on. Once those factors are checked out, then they'll proceed to dive deeper and further into the other realms to detect if it's something paranormal related.

The next morning all seemed well, but then out of

nowhere it started up again. My throat felt like it was physically closing up, so I went to the Doctor. He ran all sorts of medical tests, and ultimately said everything was fine and didn't see anything physically wrong. I took his word for it and used that to give me some peace of mind. However, later in the day it started coming up again moving in and out. I thought, "Something is definitely going on here."

I tried to psyche myself out by going with what the Doctor said and figured maybe it'll just go away. The next day I could feel my throat closing up in a stronger way to the point of being unable to breathe all over again. Gasping for air I opened the windows wide not knowing what was going on. Debating whether to call an ambulance, I knew I was in the midst of a full blown panic attack. I've had panic attacks before and know what they're like, although they're infrequent and brought upon by PTSD triggers connected back to childhood, but there was no situation that happened around that time that could have brought upon the PTSD.

The next morning the throat area was continuing to tighten again, so I went back to the Doctor and spoke to a different Doctor to a get a second opinion. She ran tests with her medical assistants as well and they found nothing physically wrong. She said, "All of your tests came back perfect." She sat back staring at me dumbfounded wishing she could give me the cause, but the cause wasn't physical and she's a physical human Doctor.

I finally did what I should've done right away as I usually do in those unexplainable events. I connected to God and my Spirit team to find out what was going on. This was a tougher case where I needed to stop and stand strong back into warrior mode. I took a deep

STAY CENTERED PSYCHIC WARRIOR

breath in and they flushed around me. They pulled me backwards to the days before earlier in the week and circled the specific mediumship reading I did on the teen suicide.

They explained I went in too deeply for too long in a state that was not centered enough at that moment. And I knew this going into it, but I broke one of my rules and made a rare exception because it was a young person. I wanted to help and thought it's no big deal I do this all the time. This was a different circumstance where it became a big deal that it had a dangerous after effect. The teenager's soul had not only latched onto me, but there was darkness present and this darkness attacked my mind blocking me from considering calling in my Spirit team when I normally would've right away in a situation like that. Looking back on it I thought that was strange. I mumbled, "I don't understand why I didn't call them. I usually do."

This goes back to me saying earlier in the book that the Darkness will put a blindfold over you blocking what it can. As I typed that out I just remembered in *The Conjuring*, the Medium was blindfolded by a dark entity from seeing one of the missing clues that wasn't coming up in the case she took.

I then stood up with complete intent and called in Archangel Michael and said, "Okay, I don't know what went wrong, but this kids energy has obviously stuck to me that I haven't been able to breathe properly ever since. You've got to get his energy off me. This means he was never in the Light. That Darkness has continuously been grabbing my throat. Please bring him into the Light now."

At that moment after days of the on and off strangulation, I suddenly felt it start to evaporate and experienced a lightening of my soul. I glided my hand around my throat in disbelief realizing that it was gone. My ego mind was still unsure of whether or not I was out of the woods, since I had just been through a several day work out, therefore I took it slowly the way you would after a bad fall. As each day continued on I noticed it truly was gone. As it stands, this teenager's soul is safe and in the Light surfing at a pristine paradise looking beach with several prominent planets in the vibrant sky close by. He has never been happier.

There are so many people in the world conducting readings now, both psychic and mediumship. There are also those fear based warnings from religious groups that connecting with spirit brings in evil. While that is not entirely true you do open yourself up for an attack. I've been an experienced psychic vessel for as long as I've known. This is with the natural ability to go deep into different areas of all worlds that exist with little to no issues. This doesn't make me susceptible to predators, which is why I normally don't do it unless necessary.

In this particular case, I felt bad that this was a young person and I wanted to get in there and help. While I received answers through that process, the soul grabbed onto my light and physically affected me. Practicing safe psychic and mediumship habits needs to be taken seriously, including by me. You want to make sure you're not carelessly doing it as that can blind you making you unaware you've invited in something more sinister into your life.

For anyone that sees mediumship, fortune telling, and psychics to be the Devil's work and to steer clear of that, understand you are connecting with spirit without realizing it. Many of your actions are divinely guided by spirit without you knowing it.

When I was four years old I was seeing and hearing

spirit without trying. This ability has never stopped since. It's not something I've had to conjure up. It's always come in on its own while I'm busy working away on other things. It can attract in darker spirits, but it also attracts in the Light as well too. With any practice you want to use discernment and pay extra caution when diving into anything. As an experienced professional, I knew going in that I was not ready that night, but I did it anyway. This contributed to the attack taking place. This is one of the many reasons I don't usually attempt to read or conduct a deeper mediumship connection unless I'm in a centered space. I knowingly walked right into one of my own warnings. How often do we break our own rules in life only to see it backfire causing us to kick ourselves later?

Souls that have passed on have been entering a Medium's psychic senses since Earth's conception. Mediumship is one of the basic ways of communicating for a soul, yet this faded over the centuries as the darkness of human ego rose to prominence cutting off the connection with all things beyond the physical. Mediumship rose to popularity again as a fad around the 19th Century.

The second you read words like, "claim" or "purported" when dealing with psychic phenomena or mediumship, then that is when you should move on to another source. There are websites that do not properly or efficiently relay information they have no business conveying. It's not a subject they are versed in enough to be discussing. They've never practiced or dove into it to understand it.

There have been numerous incidents happening since childhood and onwards where I was aware of an afterlife, although as a child I didn't know that was an afterlife. I didn't have a word for it. I just knew that the people communicating with me through the veil were not on the Earth plane. They were protective and telling me things that were coming true. I didn't think ghosts, spirits, psychic, Heaven, or any of that. There were no labels for it, but I just knew they were good and they were not human beings. I knew they were good, because I had encountered the bad ones and I can tell the difference.

There are people that strongly advise against mediumship or connecting with any spirit being. They claim that the spirit being can be a demon or devil in disguise, which can happen, but those same people wouldn't know the difference because they've spent years and decades communicating with demons unaware they were. You have to utilize safe psychic practices by honing in on who is good and who is bad, the same way you would with anyone you come across.

The endless information, guidance, and messages my own Spirit team has shown since childhood has been all the convincing I've needed. I would need to be convinced because my personality doesn't take something on face value without confirmation and the data being there. I couldn't do what I do without knowing for sure. I can't even be half sure. It has to be 100% or I'm not on board. I've been convinced enough by doing the work that it can't be explained away.

CHAPTER EIGHT

Near Death Experience Transformation

Those around me have mentioned to others that I've changed more than anyone they know. I recall a longtime friend at a dinner party talking to a professor nearby where I was standing. She said, "Out of all the people I know, Kevin has changed more times and more than anyone I've ever seen."

When I first started hearing that said repeatedly throughout my twenties I had a detachment to it. After considering it and sifting backwards over the years with everything I had been through and endured, I saw what they all meant. I've been through an endless number of healing and transformations on various levels that according to them it's more than anyone they've seen, heard of, or known. It doesn't mean I'm the only one like that, as I know there are others out there that have as well too, but I haven't come across them personally to date.

There are numerous factors that come into play as to why. Some of it was due to the severe traumatic ongoing abuse I endured growing up. There was the intensely traumatic childhood development, influences, unique life experiences and work history, genetics, the soul's path, the souls DNA, then you have the astrological influences on top of all that which make a complex person. I've never followed or believed in the horoscopes found in magazines, newspapers, and in other sources. I do believe in the science behind ones astrological human birth chart make-up.

Born this lifetime with the transformative planet Pluto in my 1st House of Self for the astrological lovers out there. That placement points to an individual who is repetitively changing and transforming many lifetimes in one. Revealing that is to indicate that I understand the tough feelings one goes through when moving through a healing and transformation process because that's been my entire life to date and continues to be so. I've been living it throughout my life repeatedly like a new chapter in the book that is my life.

Some of those transformations were minor yet significant, while other changes were drastic and appeared to take place over night. The drastic ones were pinnacle events that caused massive awakenings that made me see things in a different light and transforming my views entirely. The next day I started to see things with those newer eyes and moved with that change. This is part of what an awakening is. Transforming that many times in one life consists of these repeated awakenings. It's like each time it happens God is removing another blindfold off your eyes allowing you to see more than you had been seeing before. This particular blindfold he pulled off me was a massive one that kicked off the next major chapter of my life that consisted of the divinely guided books. This transformation was almost like a graduation of the previous Earthly life school run within the same lifetime.

The largest blindfold was pulled off and I clairaudiently heard, "You've graduated. It's now time to get to work." I had done the years of work preparation that led me to that moment. It's time to put the armor on and take my bow and arrow in hand and remember who I am, which is greater than I knew myself to be.

That big year was in 2010, which was full of pinnacle moments that ultimately dramatically altered me into who I've become today. In March of 2010, another love relationship ended that was intended to go the distance, but didn't due to the other partner's free will choice to sabotage the connection due to insecurities and low self-esteem of feeling unworthy of the connection no matter how much convincing of worthiness I offered. You cannot be in a successful long term love relationship if you're not in a place of contentment where you are independent on all levels. You might be in that space, but if the partner you've matched up with is not, then you will run into issues.

The person I was with was doing this push and pull flip-floppy behavior for years, wanted to go, wanted to stay, all the while chatting it up and messing around with other people because the insecurities and low self-esteem was that low. I had also learned that being with someone like me who can sometimes come off way too independent and confident that it will crush someone in the vicinity that feels unworthy to that. I can't be anything I'm not or pretend to not be confident, nor can I pretend to have low self-esteem to appease someone else when I don't. I've noticed those that wrestle with that tend to be offended by someone with confidence, when the higher self would see that as an opportunity to be inspired into confidence too.

Over the many years prior I had been through so many similar relationships like that with many people that this particular one was the last and final straw. I had enough of the failed relationships and reached the point of being exhausted over it. I made a soul pact that I would never get involved with another person in a serious romantic long-term relationship unless I knew for sure they were spiritually and independently ready. They would need to be on my level, or higher, or at least thriving for spiritual soul evolving greatness, because anything less than will bring about the same issues that were a clear repeated pattern. I said, "The pattern stops now. It's over I'm done."

This was my official pact prompting another change to be implemented right away. It was this firm lesson from this particular failed relationship that put me through the emotional ringer that started to ignite the big transformation that was coming up later in the year. I sensed a rumbling within me that indicated something major was coming that year, which included me psychically seeing my father's death.

Months of healing and transforming went by, then days into November 2010 I had experienced a work out injury that caused me immeasurable pain for several weeks. There was an unseen tiny tear in the male area at the back of the testicle within the tube. You might thank me for not getting anymore graphic than that, but this injury taking place is important to note as I'll illustrate.

This tear eventually caused an infection internally in

that area, all of which was causing this perpetual excruciating pain. I could barely walk because each step made the pain worse. I did not initially know where it was coming from or what it was. A growing fear over the pain developed because it wasn't going away, but was getting worse, so I connected with my Spirit team to show me what it was. They showed me that it took place when I was weight lifting during a regular exercise routine days before. They revealed that it wasn't life threatening, but could be chronic if untreated for a prolonged period of time. They explained at the time that it was an infection that needed antibiotics for the physical body.

I went to my Doctor and mentioned that I knew what it was, but many Doctors don't like it when the patient protests to know more than they do about an issue they're experiencing. He wanted to run tests and gave me worst case scenarios. This caused a three week delay in trying to get me to a Urologist.

Both Wise Ones and Claircognizant people tend to come off like big know it all's about everything, which rubs the insecure the wrong way, while others are more receptive to it since nine times out of ten the person has a point. They make you think and consider things the ego may not see or shuns. I love listening to lectures by Claircognizant people as it's so much knowledge and a different point of view I'm absorbing.

My Doctor recommended a Urologist, which scared me so I put it off another week. After three weeks of pain, I made an appointment with the Urologist, which wouldn't be for another several days. Throughout this pain, there was a moment when I could feel my conscious cutting in and out of death in a more severe way than I had experienced before. Between that and the pain, I Clairaudiently heard a rising buzz like electrical cackling sound followed by a bright flash through my Clairvoyance psychic clair sense channel that expanded wide. This caused me to detach completely from my body, which some might call Astral Travel.

Suddenly I was soaring over huge white fluffy clouds and feeling weightless and pain free. There was no fear or anxiety anymore, but complete feelings of joy, love, and serenity. I could see figures standing over these clouds as I soared past them. I later knew they were the additional guides prepping to join me on Earth soon. I saw a super tall lamppost in the distance that towered over the others. As I flew closer towards it, I saw that it wasn't a lamppost, but the Archangel Michael who I had communicated with on occasion, but not daily at that point yet. He had tinges of white, gold, and violet light that radiated around him. He was bright, strong, and marvelously large with a breathtaking presence. Without opening his mouth I could hear him say through telepathy, "We're working on it."

In Heaven, telepathy is one of the primary ways that souls communicate to each other. This is also why you cannot hide anything from one another while in Heaven, not that anyone is trying to do that. They're not human beings on Earth!

As soon as Michael said those words, I heard this electricity crackle and buzz again, then I was back on the bed facing upwards. The pain from the injury that had turned into an infection was slightly lightened, even though I could still feel it, but it wasn't as severe as it was the weeks before.

I smiled and telepathically said, "Thank you."

I sat up and looked around in stunning amazement. My spiritual sight had opened up more than it ever had. I was seeing everything differently. It was like the volume was cranked up more than it had been before. What seemed to change beyond the psychic sight was that there was a download of information planted into my psyche, because I was knowing more than I had before that moment. Without debating on it I already knew it was to be used on this next chapter of my life.

I could now see this next chapter coming since my psychic senses had also cracked open even more than they had been the years prior. The years prior the psychic hits were already off the charts, but after this particular notable night they grew stronger than before. There was a reason they did that then. It was because we all knew I had to use this Divine download to access the endless information that would be jotted down in the endless catalogue of books that would need to be written as fast as possible. Time cannot be wasted on Earth floundering. We've already lost years of not doing that since I kept procrastinating and operating on free will choices that caused delays pushing it out further. This is why you want to get to work on your purpose right away. Don't wait and keep putting it off until, until, until. Because when you do that, then it may never happen. Don't work on your purpose for a couple weeks, then push it aside because you don't feel like it for several months. We cannot afford to dilly-dally aimlessly for a long period of time. I sound like I was born in 1913 by using that word.

The next morning I was set to see the Urologist that examined me. In less than sixty seconds, after more or less feeling me up, he said something like, "You have epididymis, which is an infection. It's typically common among sports figures. All ages can get it, but it's predominately men in their twenties. All you need is a ten day antibiotic."

Bam! I know. Sometimes delays regarding what you'd like to see happen can be God delaying it, but in this case it can be due to human beings free will choice.

I was not in my twenties when this happened, but thirty-seven. Mentioning that to hammer home that friends of mine in their twenties have always had this saying that I run circles around them physically. They've claimed they've never seen someone as fit in older age. There was one circumstance when I was forty when I was jogging back to my house. A neighbor in his twenties outside shouted hi to me. I went in the house, then emerged with my bike over my head. He saw me come back out and said, "Kevin!" And with shock, "You just came back from a jog and now you're going to bike?" He stood there in disbelief, "I need to be more like you."

The fact that I received this tear infection that is mostly common with men in their twenties speaks volumes to this. The physical activity I enjoy also points to warriors that have this internal push to dive forward physically no matter what age they are - pending they can still physically move. Many of them wind up physically fit on some level well into older age.

Each day after the official medical diagnosis the pain grew less and less. This was after three weeks of non-stop excruciating pain that traveled from the source and up my body.

CHAPTER NINE

A Warrior Breaks Through the Rubble

Days into healing and weeks from the near death experience that cracked my consciousness open wider, there was another incident that popped up that would slam the psychic channel open the widest it had ever been at that point. It's unusual for that to happen as it is, but to happen twice in one month, it was clear to me that God's plan was in motion and He was not backing down whether I liked it or not.

It was 7:30 the Monday morning of November 29, 2010 when I received a call from my youngest sister who was fifteen at the time. She was crying, which shocked me because she never cries. She has always been emotionally strong. She had every reason to be crying this time as I was able to make out through her words that our father wasn't breathing.

I said, "I'm on my way."

I raced over to find him on the floor. Shouting over each other to revive him were his final life partner girlfriend with a mutual friend of ours who later became a spiritual teacher and healer. I looked up behind them and saw my father standing there with Archangel Azrael looking down at them.

I calmly said, "He's gone."

They couldn't hear me as they were rightfully in panic mode. When they heard me repeatedly say he was gone, then his girlfriend had shouted, "No!"

He had passed away suddenly at age sixty-one of heart failure. The non-stop stress in his life, which he was unable to control caught up with him. Heart failure is one of the leading causes of death now in the United States alone. It was once Cancer, which fell to number two. They both seem to take turns for that top spot. It's no surprise that heart failure is top dog in taking human lives at this point again. Earthly lives today are full of abnormal stress from stressful commutes, to stressful jobs, to stressful personal lives, to stressful people, as well as poor diets and erratic emotional states. Even if someone eats healthy, are you exercising regularly and living a life that's stress free? Stress is not just anxiety based emotions, but it can be any negative emotion such as worry, depression, sadness, or anger - all of which are creating stress. Reading negative media also adds to stress on your body, which can be detected by how angrily one reacts to a story.

This is another reason Spirit has had me talk about many of these things I do throughout our work together. This isn't to wag the finger at someone and take away someone's fun, but it's so you can live a long enjoyable life clear minded, which I have to say has been so much more pleasing to me than waking up in my own vomit from a night of partying in my early twenties. I've lived consuming toxins in high amounts and it never made me happy, nor does getting stressed out over things beyond my control. This is another reason others have commented that I seemed to be strong and calm while others are frantically falling into dramatics.

Warriors are trained early on to be warriors. Your soul endures abnormally tough and often violent circumstances for a reason. Not many souls can withstand that kind of harshness. I was thrown into it, because God apparently believed I could handle it to get me to the accelerated hierarchy he was aiming me towards. It's not something I wanted and I would never want to repeat that horror, but for Him I will do it since He clearly believes in me enough. God will not throw things at you to do or to endure that He doesn't believe you can handle first. Even if you believe you cannot handle something, He believes you can and that you will survive it, and that will get you to where He wants you to go to next.

After that big November 2010 situation with the near death experience and my father's death, my mother later randomly told me that she had a Clairvoyant nightmare where I died the night she discovered I had this near death experience. She said at the time she was so scared when she woke up from that dream. She didn't tell me as she didn't want it to be true or cause needless worry. We were both stunned at the timeline of events where she received that dream, which coincided with the same night I died only to come to and wake up spiritually transformed. My views were changing dramatically from that point on.

She and I also came to the conclusion that the death

133

she saw in her nightmare was my partial near death experience. I call it a partial near death experience, because it wasn't something that lasted for hours. It seemed to take a few minutes. When I came to consciousness, my human nightmare was ending. One part of my life was coming to a close, which included this three week injury pain in the male region, followed by the near death experience, and then my father's death all within weeks of each other.

In the Tarot, the *Death* card is symbolic for myself for November 2010. The card rarely indicates a human death, but a metaphorical one, although in this case it was death all around. It is a concrete ending to one way of life as you transform into a new one. The door to the previous way of life will be slammed closed abruptly, because something more extraordinary is coming next.

The morning my father passed away I stood there in the living room and could Clairaudiently hear the sound of shackles and handcuffs being clanked opened. My eyes looked around me as there was no one around to make that noise. I turned my wrists over and looked on in amazement as I saw white golden light around it and then around my ankles where the shackles were. I was confused for a moment because I had no idea there were etheric restraints on there until then. I felt this surging uplift and the veil fully opened up. I looked around with my mouth half open stunned as I pushed my hand through this visual paradise around me that was from across the veil at my home in Heaven. I didn't have to ask what was going on, because I knew. I clairvoyantly saw me gliding around ferociously strong in warrior hunter mode alongside with what looked like a Unicorn on the Other Side. I had never believed in Unicorns until I could see them in Heaven. The creatures that some believe to be mythological actually exist back home. Believe me I never thought I'd one day be saying those words until the visions kept coming in following the transformation.

After my father passed away, my Spirit council showed up with additional members that were joining the team. These were the beings that were standing by on those clouds during the near death experience. They basically said that I was no longer allowed to make any more excuses. I had to begin the process of moving into the next chapter, which was a big one where I had to work extremely harder than I ever have for God. This means doing one of the major things I agreed to do in my soul contract. This was the teaching and writing work. I came here for many reasons, but that was one of the bigger reasons.

I needed to come here in a human body in order to physically write out what they guided me to. This would be stuff about them. It would be stuff about Heaven, the esoteric, the metaphysical, the unknown, the philosophical, the practical, the spiritual all combined in order to start doing my part to contribute in changing one person positively at a time. If no one is being changed, I know I am being changed as each book is written.

Naturally it doesn't mean everyone would be changed over night, nor will everyone resonate with the work, but those guided to it and on the precipice of a bigger change in their life would. As my Spirit team had insisted, especially the younger ones coming up that are being brought up in a hostile world created by the generations passed. They will stop this cycle with them.

Spirit doesn't want to be talked about for the sake of bravado or gratification. It was because the work they were going to help me do was our effort in improving the state of humanity one person at a time. Maybe only one person will read one of the books, but they are absorbing that into their consciousness. Over the course of human history long after I'm gone, the number of people reading the Divine words to help life on Earth progress would eventually be in the millions on up into infinity. This would continue indefinitely since the work created are footprints that don't exist in fleeting sound bites and clichés in social media posts. The works would forever be available in the centuries to come. All of it is intended to improve the state of humanity and the progression of God's house - the planet Earth.

You help one person gain something positive from one of the books that it kicks off their change, which kicks off another persons positive change until it creates a wave of positive movement. This won't happen over night since Rome wasn't built in a day. It may take a century or more, but that's why the books will forever be available long after I've left this plane and gone back home.

This change that was coming brought in numerous members in Heaven joining my Spirit council later in the game at the time I would need them for this. One of them is Saint Nathaniel. He was one of the task masters that pushed me at that point, which was how I knew it was time. My father metaphorically held down my soul by weights during the severe traumatic training. The moment he passed away, I Clairaudiently heard those shackles being unlocked and my soul lifted up. This kicked off the spiritual writings as well as my positive internal soul engines moving into accelerated evolving mode.

One of my best friends has brought up the eerie changes that seemed to take place for me that month in November 2010. He's been around me since 2003 and remembered that year in particular. He's forever pointed out the uncanny phenomenon of the work out injury, the near death episode, my father's death, and then me choosing to go public with the spiritual stuff that I kept just for close friends and family up until that point throughout my life.

When Saint Nathaniel first introduced himself to me, he just called himself Nathaniel for several months. His tone and language was more authoritative and commanding than the other guides in my council. He also sounded older and wise by using ancient archaic language, which stood out to me. He took the helms of pushing me with the metaphysical related content. He deals with the serious humanity messages since he has great disdain for the state of humanity, but like all Heavenly beings he wants it improved. The different guides in my council are expertise in certain areas of the writings. There is also one that handles the healing information, which is why that's softer than the harsher blunt tone of Nathaniel's messages. All of this we interweave with one another, which is why the tone of a piece can shift from one sentence to another.

Humanity has the capacity to reach vast spaces of knowledge. I've forever had a hard time understanding why many are limited in consciousness when they have the ability to access it. Part of that is due to the numerous blocks around their life and not pushing themselves to explore and learn things beyond what they're capable of understanding. I've had to learn to have compassion and sympathy that everyone is at different levels of soul development and they cannot help it at that time in their life. During my drug and alcohol phase, I was still conscious enough of what was out there and knew I would be tackling it in a big way when I was done being a young rebellious punk, although there are still some element remains lingering from that.

Over time Nathaniel would reveal additional information about himself when I began persistently pressing for it. One of the first things I remember him telling me was that he was in a book that's popular on Earth. Telling me this information told me nothing.

I asked Nathaniel who he was because he sounded different than the others. It seemed like he came from a dimension that was further away than my main Spirit team. It was not the same place they are in, which is how I realized that angels reside in a different sphere of consciousness and dimension that feels closer to Earth.

He said his name is Nathaniel. This went on for months until one day he randomly blurted out that his name is Bartholomew, which confused me because it was the same voice. I was trying to get him to tell me more info about him. He persisted that he is in ancient texts and that he lived on Earth before. This still didn't tell me anything.

It was another six months in when he said he's known as a Saint on Earth. I said perplexed not believing it, "A Saint? Hmm."

I took that info he gave me and investigated to see if anything came up. I went directly to it in shock when everything he had been telling me over the many months matched up to the biblical text. The ancient text he said months before I later discovered was in the Bible. He never said Bible, he just said ancient text. And he didn't tell me right away because I had to discover it in time. God and Spirit don't like to divulge everything right away. It's either on a need to know basis or when they feel you're ready. It's the same way that some want to know their guide and angel's name. Guides and Angels don't see it as necessary to know at the time it's being asked just to know it.

I realized that Saint Nathaniel was sometimes known as Bartholomew and that he was one of the Apostles in the Bible. Jesus had described him as someone who was incapable of deceit. Nathaniel was and is still a Wise One. He's also a gifted astrologer and astronomer. Some claim that God is against astrology and astrologers, yet the man that brought Jesus gifts was an astrologer and Jesus was a gifted compassionate psychic.

When I had my near death experience it wasn't like that confirmed Heaven for me. I've always had that confirmation repeatedly enough from my own Spirit team over the course of my life. The near death experience did greatly transform me down the path of aggressively getting to work on my higher purpose. Before that moment I was procrastinating or rebelling.

In 2010, my soul burned down to the ground. When 2011 started, my fist punched upwards through the ground and I rose up out of the ashes. This change was so massive that everyone around me noticed. They were shocked to see it because the change was so transformative more than any other they noticed. Acquaintances that did not know me well walked away. They were turned off by it since they were not believers of an afterlife or of God, and I was growing more vocal about it than I ever had. While others moved with that change in me and adapted to it. Most of them ended up absorbing the change and began evolving themselves into more spiritual people. These were friends that had never uttered a spiritual word. I was soon finding out they were diving into spiritual interests. The transformation I was going through was having a positive effect with those close to me. Eventually, I'd discover it would have a positive effect with readers around the world too.

Today we hear about so many people having near death experiences to the point that it might make someone question that. How do all of these people have near death experiences now? There are more people having near death experiences than are being recorded. You may have had one and are not even aware that you did. People are having near death experiences while dreaming and not aware that they had temporarily died for a blip. Usually the near death experience is so slight it might feel longer than it actually was. That would be impossible because if you're dead for too long, then you just stay dead.

You would know it was a near death experience if it transformed you over night. This is where you were one way the day before, but after the experience your interests dramatically changed for good. Many friends you once connected with will feel like strangers you can no longer relate to anymore. The job you loved up to that date suddenly means nothing to you. The following year you end up making massive changes in your physical life to compliment the change, because continuing on with the way things are would crush your life force. You're a different person now and there's no going back. Your world turns upside down in a sense during that transformation where you're questioning everything around you including yourself. With that comes immense responsibility as to how your going to do what you were called here to do. This was also witnessed in the earlier film example in *Hereafter*. The female lead is on vacation when a Tsunami hits the village causing her to hit her head against a car in the water that leaves her unconscious. Something changes in her near death experience and psyche at that moment. She's found and dragged out of the water and brought back to life, but her perception has widened and she is no longer the same person. What follows with her story from that point is everything we mentioned about questioning it all.

There was endless media talk of the end of the world in 2012. I couldn't believe how out of control everyone was getting with that. I had said before that time there would be no end of the world on or around 12/21/12. It's just more fear based superstition. What I did say was that the years between 2010-2012 were significant not only for myself, but it was the ending of an era. Following 2012, there would be a gradual increase in others having spiritual awakenings and transformations. They would be rising into themselves and realizing there is more to Earthly life than the practical mundane set up that human beings created. They would be working to expand their consciousness in a bigger way than they ever have. We've been witnessing that happening more than in the centuries past, so the end of 2012 was the ushering in of a New Dawn. This doesn't mean it will be easy with the antagonistic Darkness in the way, but we are all strong enough to take it.

CHAPTER TEN

The Hall Of Records

and the Heaven and Earth Parallels

Through the tunnel and the crystalline shielded veil and onto the Other Side in Heaven where the layers of dimensions are broken out like the Continents on Earth that continue on in an unlimited eternity of bright worlds that some souls have yet to experience. Honing down to one area of Heaven is one of the many popular soul destinations of higher learning. It's not the same kind of higher learning on Earth, but the concept of visiting a place to gain additional knowledge is similar. As mentioned earlier, Earth is a place created in a way that would be familiar to souls. These are those Earthly wonders that no human being created, which are solely part of the Earthly mass like jungles, waterfalls, gardens, beaches, deserts, mountains, and on into infinity. In Heaven, those things exist, but on a much grander experience than the human mind can comprehend. Everything on the Other Side is much more vivid because the psychic senses are brought up to the 100% mark, so it all looks like an intensely rich picturesque paradise that is keener than any nirvana on Earth. Why would Earth be more magnificent than Heaven?

Earth would look more like a paradise if it weren't for the lack of disregard of the planet. Entire cities on Earth are saturated in a dark layered mass that is not to be confused with the heavy dirty pollution emitted from human beings. This dark mass is ethereal in nature that is puncturing in from the Darkness plane. It's drawn in by the energy on Earth making people an easy feeding ground for the Darkness. They are like vultures circling above its prey. The Angels attempt to create as much of a shield as possible, but it's a struggling fight.

In the higher learning part of Heaven, the structures are a striking white color. When I use the word striking it doesn't give it justice, but the white is not the kind of white we see on Earth. If you experienced that on Earth you'd walk onto the grounds smiling with wonder. You might say, "Oh my God, why does this feel so amazing to me right now. I just feel incredibly great inside being here."

All of the colors in the different realms in Heaven are vibrant, pristine, bright, cheerful, and uplifting this way. There is a warm feeling all across all of Heaven including in the Higher Learning facilities, which you would think would be corporate and cold like, except it's the extreme opposite of what it's like on Earth. In Heaven, everyone is unbelievably loving and pleasant in that space. I'm now being reminded of that silly, but enjoyable fictional

comedy called *Defending Your Life*, with Meryl Streep and
Al Brooks. The film is fiction and nothing like Heaven,
but what I didn't find fictitious was that everyone in the
film was exceedingly friendly in an overblown way of
course. In Heaven, everyone is warm, loving, pleasant,
and friendly, but it's not a fake inflated friendliness the
way it might be on parts of Earth, but a genuine
authentic one.

In the Higher Learning part of the realm there are
quite a bit of older appearing men and women with long
white hair and white robes. Like all souls, they can
morph into how they choose, but this is one of the
appearances they tend to take on amongst the various
councils while in this sector of Heaven. This appearance
is somewhat like the character Gandalf in the *Lord of the
Rings*, or Albus Dumbledore the headmaster in the
wizard school in the *Harry Potter* films.

Walt Disney was a popular genius Wise One that
brought pleasurable enjoyment to the masses that have
continued on long after he departed this Earth. You
have to note the uncanny irony that he seemed to pass
away about eleven years after his creation of Disneyland.
He was around long enough to get it going in a big way,
then he assisted others on Earth from his position on the
Other Side to keep it thriving. This was by working
through them psychically. He didn't like to refer to
Disneyland as an amusement park, but as the Happiest
Place on Earth. He had a dream that people from all
walks of life could come together and enjoy themselves in
a place that he received guidance from above on. I
always found it interesting to see some of his creativity
show up like his infamous castles and waterfalls flowing
down from Matterhorn mountain. This reminds me of
one part of Heaven over in the Wise One realm on the
Other Side that is filled with castle like structures built

around beautiful picturesque towering mountains and waterfalls.

There are many differing soul breeds of Wise Ones that exist. In this particular higher learning section is where some of the higher council Wise Ones are. Wise Ones are those stern exceptionally intelligent teacher types. Stern should not be misconstrued as mean. Many of those breeds of Wise Ones are part of the different councils over there.

I talk about the many breeds of Wise Ones in my book *Realm of the Wise One* because it's part of my soul tribe of people. This isn't to plug another book, but because my Spirit team and I write so much information, there is absolutely no way it can all fit into one book. I have to refer others to a different book that focuses on a specific discussion or topic IF they're interested in reading more about that. If they're not, then disregard it and keep on trucking along.

There are numerous branches within the Wise One realm, but regardless of the breed that particular Wise One is they have numerous things in common. One of them is they all tend to be on the serious darker side. The darker side is not to be confused with the evil of the Darkness though. They also all have this piercing and keen intellect and acumen. They tend to be strong, unconventional, and completely opposing to Earthly norms. When people meet them they immediately know this is someone that is different than other people. Their opinions can be so strong and blunt that it will cause offense in the easily rattled groups, but the Wise Ones don't care if someone is offended. They stand by their statements with no interest in popularity or being loved. Many that have incarnated from the different realms in Heaven tend to be on the individualistic side, but it's only alternative compared to what human ego trained society to do and believe in. In Heaven, this nonconformist way isn't seen as eccentric, because it's the way it is without question.

As a Wise One myself, I'm not part of this higher learning council, but they refer to me as one of the many warrior hunters. The warrior hunters still have what we could call on Earth the Wise One DNA, so they have the same traits that all Wise Ones have. The hunters are warriors and not like the hunters we know on Earth to hunt animals, but they are exceptionally physical, protective, self-preserved, and restless inquisitive spirits. The warrior hunters have certain personality traits that are distinguishable from others, such as they tend to move about alone and individually rather than in packs. They are also fighters of God that defend His turf and keep things in order. On Earth they tend to have a hyper alertness about them to everyone and everything around where they move about in an on guard kind of way.

Ironically, a bit of trivia, the Hunter name is like my middle name this lifetime, which is on my books. No one around me today believes that the Hunter name is coincidence, but extremely telling. In all honesty, I never considered that until it started to get pointed out by others. The Hunter name is also a family name on my Mother's side in my Earth's genealogy tree that goes back centuries.

This higher learning part of Heaven is the section that holds what they call the Hall of Records. The Hall of Records houses endless data and information on every soul that's ever existed, all lifetimes they've ever had, where they've had those lifetimes, and anything you can possibly think of is in there.

If you want to find out information about your soul,

then you would go to the Hall of Records. What you find in there is astronomically extensive. It's easier to grasp the information when you're over there. If it were here in an Earthly human made library, then we'd be sitting in there for years just trying to make sense of only some of the data. It's way too complex for the human mind at times. In Heaven, the knowledge from each of the books in the Hall of Records space are swiftly absorbed into the consciousness within a few minutes while you're in there. The information rapidly downloads into your consciousness the same way data on a computer is downloaded onto a flash drive. Every circumstance you're going through this lifetime, every challenge, every blessing, and all of your choices and non-choices, are all being recorded into your souls book that lives in the Hall of Records, which some on Earth have referred to as the Akashic Records, but it's all the same thing regardless of what you call it at anytime in history.

Your Karmic debts for mistakes are also included, and whether or not a Karmic debt was paid back or not. If it wasn't, then that would be re-added to a new soul contract as one of the things that would be re-paid back in another Earthly lifetime. If someone thinks they're getting away with murder or any other kind of soul crime, then it will have to be paid back at some point. If someone was mean to other people in any form, even if it's minor, then each time they behave that way this is added too, so be careful how you treat others. It shouldn't be surprising that everyone on the planet has something recorded in there as to how they've treated someone else at some point in their life, but the difference is that some people we know will have endless chapters filled up with that. What is also in there is if you made amends to someone you poorly treated, which helps in balancing out the Karma. This doesn't mean that you can be horrible to people as long as you continue to make amends. That's like Christians that believe they can continue sinning as long as they ask for forgiveness each time. God isn't falling for the ego's sneakiness. All higher evolved beings are onto you if that's what your plan is. The entire contents of your Soul's journey to date is in this book. This includes all soul lifetimes past and in any other dimensions you resided in.

When you cross back over to the Other Side the self-judgment process where you are judging yourself takes place in a similar facility where you go through every shred of both the good and bad you did or said, as well as what others did or said to you. Contrary to certain religious beliefs, God is not judging you, but you are judging your soul for the purpose of learning from your mistakes. If the mistakes a soul made were so great on Earth, then it will be going back for another do over. The soul is not ready to graduate upwards and onwards in those cases. Exceptions would include that if someone did horrible things, but paid for their crimes on Earth while atoning and feeling ongoing genuine remorse within their soul, then they do have a chance to graduate when they cross over. God would be the ultimate authority on whether or not a soul reached those evolving pinnacles. Humankind functions on moral authority on crimes, but it is the Divine that knows if the person displaying ongoing positive changes as a result of their crimes would allow them that rarity of soul redemption.

One thing to note is that no soul on Earth can access another person's Akashic Records without permission being granted by that other person. Even if they were granted permission, it would be impossible to obtain even half a percentage of whatever it is you're looking for. The most psychic person will have trouble getting full access to that no matter much they try. They find a few key standout things, but that's about it. One needs the out of this world psychic prowess that is only expanded to the fullest degree possible while back in Heaven in order to be able to access every detail. You can however access information from your own records, but even that takes exceptional concentration just to get a sliver of it. The human mind part of the soul has endless restrictive barriers preventing that information from pouring through.

The libraries that human beings created on Earth came from Divine guidance. The Hall of Records in Heaven is like a library that every soul is aware of back home. That other genius Wise One Benjamin Franklin, was known as one of Earth's great inventors. This guy truly used his time on Earth for positive awesomeness. He had a limited education that ended when he was about ten years old, but like many Wise Ones he was mostly self-taught. He taught himself to read, write, and then eventually created a printing company that went on to be a successful publishing house that published all sorts of materials and books. He wrote clever motivational pieces in Almanacs. He also brought in the lending library to people, even though libraries date back to the Greek days, but they were restricted to "special" members. Benjamin was one of the ones that brought it to the general public to be able to borrow books. He received the Divine guidance from above for all of this, then it was set in motion. His achievements in inventing were so massive that they are still used today. We wouldn't have some of the many human luxuries we take advantage of today had it not been for him.

Benjamin also helped bring electricity to human life, and he was one of the Founding Fathers that helped write the Declaration of Independence. He was an author as many Wise Ones are because they can teach, preach, and be as long-winded as they like with no one to stop them. It's no surprise that Benjamin Franklin's image is on the American currency $100.00 bill. This is unusual considering that this is typically bestowed on Presidents. He was one of the few exceptions because of the many critical inventions he brought to humanity.

This is to give you an example of someone who took advantage of his human life and got to work as quickly as possible. He was accessing incredible Divine guidance information from wise council members in Heaven in this place of higher learning.

PAST LIVES

All past lives your soul has had are also in your personal chronicles in the Hall of Records. There can be a connection between someone's great love or passion for something this lifetime that can often be traced back to a past life connection.

I've always had a strong bond for all things nature related, but that's because it brings me peace and a stronger connection line with God. I especially have a great love for the ocean and the water. I've lived in beach cities for more than half of my life that I'm known as a beach dude.

There were at least two past life visions where I was killed while at sea. I was a sailor in one where I drowned on the ship I was on that went up in flames. In another life I was a merchant marine when I was in the boiler room and it blew up. In that one, I died at age 26, and I was also a racist homophobe. Go figure that I'd rally mobs up in hatred to go after people. Ironic that I'm the opposite of that today where I rally people up in Universal love instead. This is said to note that the same fighting nature in my personality is there, but now those gifts are used for good.

My romance with the ocean spans centuries, but I do have subconscious fears of drowning. I also almost drowned again this lifetime when I was five in the swimming pool at the apartment building we lived in at the time. I was jealous the other kids swam without a life ring, so I got rid of my life ring and floated to the bottom. I could see my mom who was there laying out next to the pool. She quickly jumped and dove into the pool immediately and pulled me out. How could I do something so senseless? I was five so I'll cut me some slack for that rash decision on my part. It's like my Moon in Aries who acts impulsively without considering the consequences. Today I take my time weighing decisions that it can aggravate some that need an immediate answer. You're thinking, "With all of these lives of drowning or near drowning, do me a favor just stay out of the water."

I've also been indifferent about past lives neither believing or disbelieving. I'll state something that I sense is a past life, but I look at that as me just interpreting what I'm getting, but my ego mind will remain in skepticism or neutral and on the fence about it. There were things about me that I've seen that strangely matched my personality from other lives, but my actions back then are actions I would never do or say today. I have friends who strongly believe in past lives and have had visions as well too. I don't credit or discredit any of that, but instead I have an open mind in that respect. I cannot get anywhere if I don't allow myself to hear all sides of a topic. I'm a sponge for knowledge, information, ideas, and the things I haven't personally experienced yet. I am not an all knowing being since that title goes to God.

I have a long history of making psychic related statements that have later come true. These are the kinds of statements that most disagreed with at the time, but they quickly grow quiet when it comes to fruition. They also learned to not doubt some of the things I say – not that I cannot be wrong on occasion. This is said as there is quite a bit of doubt from others when I make a psychic statement. They end up coming back to inform me that what I said came true, but they didn't want to believe it at the time since the prediction outcome wasn't the wish they wanted.

For the most part, the soul develops amnesia about any previous lives, even though some may sense snippets of a past life. If they knew every detail and felt every wound or mistake they made in a past life, then imagine living this life with all its challenges, and then on top of that you're burdened by something you did to someone when you were someone else in the year 1752. That would be stressful to have on your mind!

One of the few benefits to knowing about your past life is if it can help you heal what you're going through in this life, because the soul does have a connection to its past lives. You remember all your lives in full when you cross over back home. When you're back home your soul has a higher perspective. It doesn't feel negative emotions like stress, sadness, or anger while in the Light in Heaven. Therefore, it can handle all of its lives with a sophisticated emotional detachment.

PARALLELS OF THE NEVER ENDING STORY

WITH HEAVEN AND EARTH

As it may have been noticed, I sometimes love to bring up movie references to make a point or comparison because movies are so beloved by most people that it's easily relatable. Many films come from the creative filmmakers psychic intuition, which is more often than not Divinely guided regardless if they're aware of it. If they are a receptive soul, then that Divine inspiration will be dropped into their consciousness to bring knowledge or enjoyment to human beings. It's all filtering in from above. You can easily spot the ones that are incorporating Divine guidance inspiration into their art, technology, and inventions that help propel humanity positively forward or give them a sense of joy.

The Spirit council back home reminds me a bit like in the fantasy film, *The Never Ending Story*. In the movie, a fictional place called Fantasia is disintegrating and being destroyed by a dark force called, "The Nothing". This can be a metaphor for Earth, which is being destroyed by the Darkness and the darkness of ego in humankind.

In the film is a key character named Atrejo who is a youthful appearing mighty warrior hunter. He shows up at the castle where the Empress resides in Fantasia to accept the mission and purpose of fighting to save the land from being swallowed up by The Nothing. In Earth's case, The Nothing would be the darkness and the dark side of the ego that causes all of the chaos and disruption.

Heaven sends its best to Earth to incarnate in human form with missions and purposes to combat this darkness. Those people are light warriors, warrior of lights or light

153

workers or Earth Angels – all of which are the different names for the many that know they are here with specific purposes and missions. To make a point we call them Earth Angels, but back home there are no labels. These human beings are contributing their gifts and talents in their own way to help better humanity and progress Earthly living. Since one person cannot do that job, many are sent to Earth holding the various jobs they do. They could be that Incarnated Elemental person that works at an entrance booth at a National Park, to a Star Soul that helps to bring technological advances to humankind, to the Incarnated Angel that helps to motivate someone to positively change their life through their platform of choice, or to the Wise Ones that teach knowledge to help souls evolve and advance humanity forward in the process. Many of them may not be who you think they are. You may not even be aware you're in the presence of a warrior of light right away.

This same parallel could be seen in The Never Ending Story. Atreyo is known as a great warrior that the leaders know to be Fantasia's only hope to help save them. This is the same as some souls in Heaven approaching their own council back home with the mission purpose of incarnating on Earth to help contribute to it and their soul in some positive way. They know for certain duties they have to go down to Earth to do it since many people are not paying attention to their own guides, let alone knowing they have guides to pay attention to.

Atreyo arrives at the castle and moves through the crowd and approaches one of the council leaders named Carion. Carion sees that Atreyo appears athletic with a serious ferocious determination, but he along with the crowd around them are stunned because he also looks like a kid.

Carion dismisses him, "I must ask you to leave."

Atreyu says, "If you don't want me here, then you shouldn't have sent for me."

The crowd gasps in shock.

Carion taken aback in amusement, "It was not you we sent for. We wanted Atreyu, not Atreyu the child, but Atreyu the warrior."

Atreyu scoffs in that typical Wise One demeanor just before walking away from the leaders, "I am the only Atreyu with the plains people, but I'll be happy to go back to hunting the purple buffalo."

"No, wait!" Carion shouts with begging insistence. "Come back please."

Atreyu walks back up the stairs and Carion takes him more seriously. Carion says, "If you truly are the Atreyu we sent for, then you would be willing to go on a quest?"

Atreyu says, "Yes of course, what kind of a quest?"

Carion explains that it's to save Fantasia and how he will go about doing that. This is similar to the Divine council back home mapping out a soul contract for the warrior of light soul. The realm soul is different from a newborn soul's contract, because a warrior of light or an earth angel soul is usually older than their human age, which is why you hear some people calling others an Old Soul.

A newborn soul is incarnating into an Earthly life for the first time, so their soul's age is the same age as their human age. They are easy to spot because they are the ones that wreak the most havoc on Earth. They cause the most problems through perpetuating hatred, shallow superficiality, greed, drama, gossip, violence, and on and on. They can be anyone from the person that posts negative attacks or words in articles, blogs, products, companies, or on social media one after the other with no end in sight. They can be that person that judges others based on their appearances, or those good looking people that only seemed to have good looking friends because they base friendship on the superficial exterior. An evolved soul isn't looking at the exterior of a person to determine quality, but looks beneath that to see the soul. A newborn baby soul can be those in radical terrorists groups that harm and terrorize others. This is beyond Isis terrorists, but can also extend to those on social media that terrorize others through attacking or complaining words. Both have the same energy where they contribute nothing positive towards the benefit of the planet, even though they might be under the delusion they are. Attacking and bullying in any form does not come from an evolving soul. You may have lost it once in that manner, but it's not how you typically are. This is about those who do this regularly since it's their general demeanor.

There are what is known as a mid-level soul. These are the people that are living an Earthly life to gain additional lessons and growth. They might be that person that isn't wreaking much havoc, but are living a human life that is expected such as getting married, buying a house, and raising kids. All of the work and responsibilities that come with that are shaping and molding that soul in a positive way. An exception might be if they are working at a job or side passion that is benefiting humanity or improving others lives in some way. They might also have decided to come here simply to raise a child that is going to be bringing important things to humanity such as the earlier example of Walt Disney and Benjamin Franklin. One of the goals and purposes of their parents was to give birth to them.

The Warrior of Light and Earth Angel souls of the light souls tend to endure harder circumstances because they have to gain strength by breaking through that resistance. You're not going to be sent to battle without first going through some boot camp training. They know it will be difficult to do that and to have to fight to survive in the dog eat dog world that is Earth. It may require them to be born in an unpleasant situation to having to slum it in a day job they don't like for awhile. This is knowing they have a greater purpose they need to get to work on. If they are truly the light soul that is called on, then to make the purpose happen they will either find a way or they will make one. They're basically not sitting ducks unhappily working this job and doing nothing about it. It's not that they dislike the day job because it prevents them from living in a lap of luxury accomplishing nothing. It is that they know they have to get to work on what they agreed to do while here. I've witnessed many around me that were stuck in these day jobs, then broke away able to work for themselves, start their own business, or work from home. By all means they didn't move to the latter to have fun. In fact, they were suddenly working from morning until night because they enjoyed this new work situation that is their life purpose. Doing what they love while simultaneously being a positive benefit to others.

In *The Never Ending Story*, Carion tells Atreyo, "To find a cure and to save our world, no one can give you any advice except this, you must go alone and you must leave all your weapons behind. It will be very dangerous."

Atreyu is strong and composed with a higher maturity than those of his same years, "Is there any chance of success?"

Carion says with discouragement, "I do not know, but if you fail our whole world will be destroyed."

Atreyu breathes in this mission feeling the weight of

it, before he warriors up with determination again, "When do I begin?"

Carion says, "Now and you must hurry Atreyu. The Nothing grows stronger everyday."

This is similar to the Heavenly soul being immediately prepped to begin their Earthly mission right away, because they know the darkness of ego and the Devil in humanity continues to grow stronger in numbers. It is virtually impossible not to see this wherever you go. The good ones threaded throughout that are those realm souls of the Light. They are also impossible to miss because they radiate higher than the Darkness.

Carion gives Atreyu a necklace with a symbol on it. He lets him know that it will guide and protect him for as long as he wears it. This is similar to the soul that incarnates on Earth who knows they must never allow their faith to falter. You must believe with all your might on where you came from. You know without a doubt that you are watched over and guided while on your mission by God by at least one main sole guardian angel and one spirit guide. You are watched over, guided, and protected. As long as you stay focused on that faith, then you can get through the challenging circumstances on Earth.

While the film is fictitious, you can see the parallels between that and a soul choosing to incarnate into an Earthly life to be of service to improve God's House and His Children in a positive productive manner. This is the same way your human parents send you off to human made schools to learn from teachers. In this case, the incarnating soul is the teacher and God is the parent bringing that teacher to the world to do their part for Him. He knows his Children won't pay attention to Him or His Angels, but they will be more likely to pay attention to a soul in a human body.

Your soul approaches the council in Heaven or the council approaches you. This is to discuss you incarnating back to Earth for different reasons. You choose to go back and work out the reasons why, your purposes and missions you'll tackle, the experiences you'll endure both challenging and not, as well as who will be assigned to you throughout your Earthly journey. All of that detail is also added to your soul's book in these heavenly records. Naturally when you head back home to Heaven and you look over your soul contract you might say, "Okay, I did that, did that, oh whoops, no I didn't do that. Ugh! And I remember that kept popping up in front of me, but I didn't put it together or act on it."

You have free will choice and are not forced to do anything since God doesn't like prisoners or controlling people, despite what some might believe on that matter. He never causes harm on other people. They do fine with that on their own.

I've had many deep conversations with others over the years. People have varying belief systems. Some believe the soul reincarnates, others believe they move onto what we call Heaven, and others believe that when you die, you die the end. Atheists tend to believe the latter. They need concrete physical tangible evidence. Forging on with faith in something they cannot see is real or not is challenging.

Having an analytical scientific mind, I'm doubtful and skeptical of anything, everything, anybody and everybody. With that said, I can't believe in an afterlife if I don't have some measure of proof that points to that existence. My proof has come through with the numerous Divine connections with beings from beyond. These are connections I've had since I was a child. It was always there as soon as I was conscious. What made me believe was that I could hear this council talking to me sounding as clear as the day as if someone is standing next to me. One could easily say those are crazy voices or your own voice, but I knew they were not. I couldn't have accomplished all I have this lifetime as a crazy person that hears crazy voices. They are in a different voice that is not mine, which is fair enough to be doubtful, but the big reveal is that these beings have told me endless things that ended up coming true. This isn't just by my account. It's also verified by those around me who've been with me forever and attested to this reality.

While growing up I didn't know what or who these beings are or were. I didn't equate them to being in Heaven or have a name for them, but I knew they were not human like me, and that they were close enough or able to get close enough that I can hear them. This coupled with the sporadic visions they've given me of the worlds beyond. The same way they've projected those visions to me, they've also projected visions that were about circumstances on Earth about to take place whether in my life or someone else's. It was in the detail of the prophecies both minor and major they've given me over the course of my life that made me understand what comes after this. Otherwise, I'd probably be an atheist or at least agnostic. My analytical mind is too powerful that it requires physical proof of something, yet it's the ethereal heavenly gifts that have proven it enough for me to believe. When I listened and followed other people in the early years, then I ended up on the broken path. When I followed God and my Spirit team more often than not, then great things started to open up. I'm going to continue following them, since they've never let me down.

CHAPTER ELEVEN

There Is No Death

There are more confirmed accounts of the likelihood of Heaven over no possibility. For me again, the personal repeated confirmations that satisfied me were from the non-stop psychic information I've received of things about to happen that would later come to fruition. There was no such thing as a good guess, because those instances were regarding information on things I wasn't asking for, considering, caring about, trying to prove anything, or wanting to know. It filtered in and I said it out loud and it later came true.

Atheist's don't believe in life after death due to their being no physical proof for them, but the contradiction for them is there is no proof that Earthly life is all there is either. If it is believed without a doubt that there is no life after death because you haven't seen it, then that is not enough validation or confirmation for those that do believe. If I didn't have deep psychic connections, I still could not imagine going through life shunning the unknown. As analytical and skeptical as my personality is, I would still be open minded to things that I didn't know or hadn't experienced. I won't discredit something because I don't know anything about it. For those that do not believe, you're not an all-powerful person who has seen everything with your own eyes. You only know what you know through physical proof, which is not enough to bank on.

Agnostics are less strict and rigid than Athiests. Agnostics may not believe in something, but they don't disbelieve either. They're on the fence and flexible to the unknown, which leaves their soul open enough to allow the Divine knowledge and awakening to come flushing through at the right time.

Ironically, those that have strong Claircognizance tend to be Athiests or Agnostics. They have more of an analytical scientific background or personality and need concrete physical proof to believe something they cannot see with their own eyes. They are receiving Divine information through their Claircognizance channel often without realizing it or considering that it is connected to psychic ability and Divine guidance. It has to come in strong enough repetitively that it triggers an awakening where they realize it could possibly be Divine oriented. However, there are numerous cases of Athiests that were strict about that belief system until something major changed that.

Lee Strobel was an Athiest journalist in the early 1980's when his wife began moving away from that and towards a belief in Christ. He scoffed and ridiculed her newfound growing belief system at first, until he realized their opposing beliefs were becoming so strong that this was serious and their marriage was going to be in jeopardy. He then privately went on a two year investigative journey of attempting to disprove the existence of Jesus Christ. He was in for a major awakening when all of those hours and months filled with endless data of Christ's existence proved him wrong. He ended up converting as a result, which can be seen in the film *The Case for Christ*.

There are stories of Athiests that were rigid with that belief system until they also had some kind of spiritual awakening that transformed them so deeply they could no longer believe there was nothing else out there. This was their personal spiritual transformation that indicated their soul was evolving dramatically at that time. When your soul, not your physical body, is connected to what's going on beyond the physical plane, then you will pick up on something that isn't of the physical world.

THE FRONT AND BACK GATE

Contrary to some scripture about sinners being sent to Hell by God, this isn't true, however one's soul could be pulled in that direction. Therefore, it's essentially the soul that is being pulled to that area automatically on its own without realizing it. It's like when you're dreaming at night and your consciousness is taking you into a nightmare you have no control over. You can pull yourself out of that nightmare through awareness of the Light. One cannot go through life feeling there is no consequence to bad behavior without trying to raise their consciousness.

The Darkness is not a place that God sends souls to. The soul has a choice to where it will be pulled and gravitated towards when it passes on. If the soul was living in Darkness and caused perpetual harm to others whether physically, emotionally, mentally, or through words, then the odds of them being pulled into the Darkness upon death are stronger.

Sometimes the harmful soul can be lifted up into the Light upon crossing over if there is any measure of Light within it, even if it's just a sliver strong enough to take over as it moves into the next plane. It helps to have some measure of faith, since it's that believing in the Light element that draws your soul into that Light.

At the same time someone can have immense faith, but if their actions, thoughts, and feelings contradict that, then that's enough for the Darkness to battle the Light to take over. This means that just because someone says they're religious, but they're running around casting judgment, then it's that hatred that is enough for the Darkness to take over. A non-believer may be a genuinely good person that had done so many great things in the generosity giving department with humanity, then that persons light is strong enough that the darkness will have a hard time getting in there.

Upon death as the soul is travelling through the tunnel to head back home to Heaven there will be two entry ways. There is a front gate and a back gate. The back gate heads to the Darkness. These gates are not visible or marked, but don't worry you cannot accidentally go through the wrong gate. Your soul will be pulled in the direction it's supposed to go depending on what kind of person you were on Earth. Mostly the back gate is reserved for the horrible people of the world. This may satisfy those that cannot imagine that someone like Adolf Hitler or Osama Bin Laden going to the same place to hang out in Heaven where Mother Teresa or Martin Luther King Jr. is. Because then that would mean there are no consequences to bad behavior. You can do whatever you like and be as mean as you want to other people because you're going to the same place, which is not true.

Those that were evil on Earth will undoubtedly go through the back gate to the Darkness. This would include abusers, haters, and harmful people. When there is that much malice in your heart and soul, then that is enough to pull someone through the back gate. The exception would be those that evolved and radically atoned and transformed becoming a model soul. Those that reject God or any idea of a higher power travel through the back gate to the Darkness on their own as well too. This isn't as punishment for not being a believer, because there are non-believers that were good people that move through the front gate into the Light on the Other Side. It is because they're rejecting of God is so powerful that the Light cannot reach them, and believe me the Light is trying. Their spiritual family on the Other Side is attempting to bring that spirit back home. A person can be a huge believer of God, but if they were evil like the terrorists that kill people for not being believers, then their soul is pulled into the Darkness. They can be a believer, but were condemning people in hatred from a Church pulpit, then they will be travelling through the back gate into the Darkness. You don't get a free pass to the Light on the Other Side just for believing in God.

There are jokes about Hell such as, "Well, if I'm going to Hell then at least everyone else will be there and it'll be a big party."

A party is hardly anything close to what happens in the Darkness. It is a place no one should want to go. After a traumatic life review in the Darkness, the soul rapidly travels right back to the Earth plane to be born into another Earthly life all over again. This time their life is fraught with even more challenges to overcome. This is not as a form of punishment to the soul, but for the sake of hoping that soul will learn something the next time around and evolve. Unfortunately, they rarely learn much the second time around either and end up repeating their Earthly lives for centuries until they're finally gotten through and begin evolving their soul, then they can finally go home to the Light. The soul is not being sent to the back gate into the Darkness by God. Their own soul is pulled into that direction on its own because of how strong the energy is within them. No one controls a soul, not even God. The soul has complete free will choice to move where it wants to go on Earth and on the Other Side. If a soul moves into the Darkness, then it does so on its own.

The tunnel to the Other Side not only contains a front gate to the Light and a back gate to the Darkness, but moving through the tunnel is also something that some souls avoid doing upon death. They may avoid moving through it out of fear or because they may not know they've died and will stay around the area they passed away in. When one dies they don't always realize they died, because when the soul separates from the body it is not a painful process. When the soul detaches from the body, it may not automatically move into the tunnel, but may instead start checking things out around them. They'll see people grieving over them and will not understand why. They may even become angry or irritated that everyone on Earth is ignoring them when they're standing right there.

In other cases this amnesia and refusal to not realize they're dead could keep them bound to the Earth plane, which is something you don't want to do either.

Eventually over time God manages to lure them into the Light, but it is not without repetitive effort. This is the same way that Guides and Angels may be trying to guide someone on Earth, but that human being isn't paying any attention to them as many do not. Imagine now you're dead, but your soul is alive, yet you don't realize you're dead, and there are higher spirit beings constantly trying to get your attention to move into the Light. They're still dealing with an Earthbound spirit, which is similar to a human being, except without the physical body. You're stuck with the same feelings you had when you were living on Earth. This is where Hauntings come in, although the spirit isn't purposely haunting a house or a location. They're unaware they've passed on. Their soul is moving through the same repetitive loop where they continue to go through the same movements and motions not breaking away from it. Those spirits are not being ignored by the Light, because the Light is aware of where they are and are attempting to lure them into the tunnel to get them back home in the Light. If a soul on Earth was oblivious to Spirit on Earth, then they would be oblivious to them while in what some call limbo or purgatory.

Not all suicides are destined to roam Hell or purgatory either. A great many suicides that were related to being depressed or suffering from a mental health issue do go to the Light on the Other Side. However, the suicides that we're done out of malice, such as those that kill themselves to prove a point the way terrorists might do, then they head through the back gate. Those that kill themselves and others such as fathers or mothers that snap and take their families lives and then themselves, they all go into the Darkness and then almost quickly back into another Earthly life. Those that murder anyone will go through the back gate, but not those that did it out of genuine self defense. I can't tell you how many people are stabbing and killing their babies and children, but the number is astronomical. Those people plagued by the Darkness will head through the back gate upon death, which is for certain. God will never tell someone to hate, harm, or hurt another person.

There is also another area that is no place for the soul. It is a space where some souls go before choosing to go through the back gate or the front gate. It is similar to purgatory or limbo as some call it. It's a place of perpetuating sadness. The issue there is they are good people, but may have been severely depressed or took their lives abruptly and were unaware they've died. They kind of shuffle around in this space with heads down and in this immense sadness not being alerted to anything. If you attempt to communicate to them they are unresponsive. That is until the Light is finally able to get through to them after numerous attempts that can go on indefinitely.

This is similar to the early story where I was at my father's house that had all of those souls that seemed to be stuck and it was physically affecting me. And also with the story I told you about where the teenager killed himself and I did the mediumship reading. The one whose soul had continued to suffocate me as a result, which he was not purposely doing. As you read also, I called in the bigger angelic guns to bring them all into the Light, which is where they are now. Unfortunately, not everyone knows to do that because they're unaware there is a lingering spirit in purgatory in their vicinity. However, the higher spirit beings continuously attempt to reach those souls to get them to wake up from their nightmare and believe, so they can go back home to Heaven where it's fun!

HUMAN DEATH

The soul is one of the most powerful entities created. You surround and enclose it with the weight of a human body, and then the soul feels like it's wearing a heavy coat drenched in water. There's going to be a sound when it's released from the confines of that dense armor upon human death. Typically, the soul spirit of the human being will exit or be pulled out through the head or the crown area of the person.

There have been numerous occasions where someone took a photo of someone immediately after they passed on. They've turned off all the lights, except some dim nightlights so it's not pitch black. These same photographers have been stunned to see a light mist above the deceased. There is no flash being used with the camera or any bright lights on in the room, then the photograph shows this dusty film over the head of the deceased. To me this further indicates the soul spirit exited through its own physical head and the transition into the Light was seamless.

Earth is one of the spirit plane levels of Hell. It is the bottom of the barrel. When your human life ends, it's like you snap awake with this crystal clear awesome clarity. This greatness makes your entire soul flood with joyful happy tears because it is that mesmeric. It's like someone turned the light on in a dark room and the volume of music is turned way up.

As your soul travels back home through the tunnel fearlessly, every sound and crackle is sharpened. Your eyes pierce into everything it looks at scanning and seeing more than what's there. The feelings experienced are enhanced, richer, and more visceral. Someone on Earth might use a toxic vice like drugs or alcohol because they want to feel good. This synthetic way of feeling good doesn't come close to the senses that awaken when you cross over. Suddenly you're alive, awakened, and re-born again. Those cravings of toxic substances aren't there anymore with your soul's newly strong heart. This is connected to your thinking processes opening up like in the films *Limitless* and *Lucy*, except it's coming upon you naturally.

Any memory you're looking for, any facts you need, your soul's mind has easy access to it. It's like an encyclopedia is downloaded into your consciousness. It's an awesome feeling that nothing on Earth can give you. Believe me I've tried through drugs, alcohol, pills, relationships, work obsessions, etc. All of that is abysmal in comparison.

When you reach the Light on the Other Side you are amazed by how awesome it is. You immediately recognize it because it's your home! It's where your soul is from. Those that are present to greet you are also people you recognize. This includes your Twin Flame split apart if they weren't on Earth, which is rare. I've heard others feel frustrated that they'll never meet their Soul Mate and Twin Flame. It pains me to hear that for numerous reasons. One of them is because you have more than one Soul Mate, but you only have one Twin Flame. Your lifelong Twin Flame is more than likely on the Other Side. Why would they come here to Earth when you spend an eternity with them back home? And when you're back home with them it's not like you're glued to the hip there either. Sorry to burst the bubble of those spending years and decades waiting around due to this romantic notion of meeting their other half Twin Flame. This is coming from me, someone who is an incurable romantic at heart, but I still recite what my guides show me and this is what they have shown regarding that.

The recent Twin Flame craze has rapidly become an Internet phenomenon in some of the spiritual communities claiming that everyone's Twin Flame is on Earth waiting to unite with them. There are so many people either waiting for their Twin Flame or believing the person they're with is their Twin Flame, when it is more than likely one of their many Soul Mates. This prompted me to reveal what my Spirit team has shown me on Twin Flames in my book, *Twin Flame Soul Connections*.

GRIEVING

The human experience can be rougher when there is loss involved with another soul, whether it is a pet, loved one, parent, child, lover, or friend. Even if one of those vanished or left you physically, but did not pass on, the loss is still equally painful. It has caused a great number of people to lose their faith and fall into a depression feeling unable to climb out of. It will make you hate or question God wondering if He even cares. He and all higher vibrational spirits do care and understand that human beings suffer in the physical world. There is no such thing as a challenge free life. They want everyone to experience peace as much as possible, so they attempt to do their best to guide the person swiftly through its life challenges to reach a state of peace. The human being can also find peace through their daily choices that bring them closer to this serenity. Spirit's perspective is extremely altered compared to the human perspective. This is because the human perspective is limited, while the heavenly perspective is broadened. All souls unite when it's there time to make passage into the other world.

Angels say you cannot ignore you when you're experiencing emotional turmoil and they're not ignoring you either in those moments. They're helping you through challenging periods in your life to help you move through the grief stages, which is normal to feel, experience, and process. There is no time limit to experiencing those things. They help move you through the experience of pain especially when you lose someone you love.

Your loved one is not truly gone even though it might feel that way because you can't see them, but you can feel them, and notice the signs your loved one is putting in your path. This is a great way for them to communicate to you. It's through ways that you would recognize them with, such as by playing a song on the radio or in a store that would make you notice. You might say, "Oh wow, this was his/her favorite song! And today would've been their birthday!"

It's through the little subtle cues you'll notice when your psychic radar is cracked open. You don't need a Medium to help you connect with them, because you have those mediumship skills built into your soul. A Medium may help confirm the signs you're getting if you feel doubtful, but you have both psychic and mediumship abilities built deep down in the pilot light of your soul.

Sometimes the signs of your loved ones presence can be so subtle that it won't be picked up on while you're experiencing heavy grief. Heavy grief and emotion is a block distracting any spirit or soul communication. As the grief lightens, then the communication grows stronger.

Deceased loved ones will stay close to the grieving during the time they are having trouble with their passing. As you grieve less they can move on to do other things while in Heaven, but they are just a Divine communication away. Whenever you need to talk to them, you can pour your heart out mentally, out loud, or in writing. Writing it out is a great way because they do read it and it also helps you focus on it with intention. You can write it out to yourself in an email or notepad and send it to yourself too.

One of the ways a spirit can communicate is also through electricity. They're able to mess with electricity and technical things to let you know they are there. It's nothing to be frightened of.

An example would be when someone close to me texted this:

"I'm sitting in my bedroom and the printer goes on in the guest room. The printer is not plugged in. I can hear it turning on and resetting and then it turned off and it was so scary. I went into the room to look at the printer and it was completely off and not plugged in. I thought that's weird. I went in there with a flashlight, and then I go back into my room and Alexa (wifi voice activated speaker) is like, "I'm sorry what did you say?" I said, "Alexa, I'm not talking to you." She said, "Oh. I'm sorry, I thought I heard my name." I was like what is going on. I went to go sleep downstairs I was so freaked out, so either some kind of electrical thing is going on inside my place or something supernatural is going on."

God and the angels are aware that human beings on the physical plane experience suffering. They know it's only temporary, even if an evil soul moves through that back gate. They will move through that perpetuating Darkness and do another repeat do over until they can get it right. In Heaven's Light, the soul gives off a radiant loving life force long after its transitioned back home. Call on Archangel Raphael daily to help heal any pain and sadness, call on Archangel Azrael to help with the grief, call on Archangel Raguel to bring justice to a situation that caused your loved ones passing.

Many turn from Heaven when they experience a loss. Why didn't an angel swoop in and help? Why didn't someone in Heaven come into help? These are questions that have complex answers, because no answer is exactly the same. It might have involved the free will choice of the soul or other souls on Earth. Spirit guides and angels are warning people of danger, but if no one is listening to them, then there isn't much else they can do. One of the many big ways Spirit can warn you is through the Clairsentience psychic clair sense. It would come in as a gut instinct or an uneasy feeling before a pending doom enters the picture.

Some pain in life cannot be avoided as it is part of the journey all souls signed up for before coming here. It is part of the growing, learning, and healing your soul will go through during its time on this planet. There is no such thing as a pain free life. It is intended to be challenging in some way. As challenging as that is to believe during a time of grief, it is part of the soul's contract. It's not something that can be understood right away, but it will as you move through the experience knowing that with every fiber of your being that your loved one is indeed with you. You can communicate to them and they will hear you.

Death is one thing that everyone on the planet can agree on and that's that everyone will pass on at some point. Because there are no pictures or physical proof, they see it as the great unknown, which can bring up fear. It's a natural process to go back home where you originated. Earth is just a temporary rental space the souls inhabit.

Crossing over back home to Heaven can be confusing for some as they may not be fully aware they passed on.

It can take some getting used to. Crossing over feels like you're waking up from a nightmare, which was your Earthly life. Even though while you may be living an Earthly life and perfectly happy, the perspective is drastically different on the Other Side that it's much better than it was on Earth.

Why doesn't God reveal Heaven or proof of life after death to every single person on the planet? The answer Spirit has said is because then people would be distracted by it and wouldn't bother getting to work. Why would they get to work when they know what clearly awaits them is their one true home where they originated from? It would defeat the purpose of their souls incarnating to this Earthly school if that information was easily accessible. Spirit shows just enough to those that can pick up on it. The stronger your psychic channels are and the more evolved your soul has transformed on its evolution, then the clearer they can see it. They won't see everything, but enough of the glimpses of it the same way psychic hits come in. It won't come in one full sweep, but through sporadic episodes the same way your human memory this lifetime can remember certain things from childhood, but not everything. If you can barely remember every detail of childhood, then how would you recall every detail of Heaven?

In Heaven, your perspective is clearer and profound. Contrary to any fears one might have about dying, it's nothing to fear, because you experience an overwhelming release from the weight of the Earth plane while you're moving through the tunnel. Life back home is much more colorful and vibrant, as well as joyful and uplifting. These are some of the endless impressions I've received through my psychic clair senses since human birth this lifetime. I've also always seen my tribe back home since there are various tribes throughout the many planes that exist within the different dimensions. The Universe, Heaven, and the Spirit Worlds are all so massive it is impossible to dissect it all in one sitting. Earth is one grain of sand at a beach compared to the endless grains of sand all throughout infinity and beyond.

CHAPTER TWELVE

I Am Psychic and So Are You!

One of the greater misunderstandings about psychic phenomena is that only a select group of people on the planet are gifted with psychic perception. Because of that belief some have either lifted psychics into special royalty status or discredited psychic foresight altogether. I am psychic and so are you! Every living breathing organism is psychic from people, to animals, to plants, and to the entire planet. Everything that is not human made, but God created, has access to these Divine communication receptors deep within the soul's DNA, regardless if there is awareness of that or not. This is one of the ways that everything and everyone is affected and connected to one another.

When you walk into a room full of people and

someone is angry and creating a dramatic scene, then every single person in that room will be negatively affected by it. I've been in restaurants where someone nearby our table has this infectious hysterical laugh that makes us and the surrounding tables light up in laughter as well too. When I was working on a film production for Warner Bros. called *"The Perfect Storm"*, I had answered my phone and it was one of the Assistant Directors calling from the soundstage. He paused moving from serious and formal to lightening and warming up to tell me, "You know Kevin, I could be having the most stressful day on set, but as soon as you answer the phone there is this sudden calmness that relaxes me. It's every single time that sometimes I'll admit I'm not calling you for anything important, but I just need to absorb some of what is coming off you. I spoke to others on set about it and they all agreed and said they had noticed the same thing too."

Back during those entertainment day job days as I called it, my boss wouldn't always take his car to work and would be driven or take public transportation, because it was less stressful. I said to him once, "I live past you now, so if there are ever days you want to ride, let me know, I don't mind I like the company."

There were days that he started to take me up on that offer. As months passed by, I ran into his husband who said to me, "I can tell the days that he rides home with you. Because those are the only days that he comes home calm, relaxed, and in good spirits."

The psychic energy that people give off and radiate transfers to other people in the vicinity. When you're radiating a serene, loving, calmness, then those around can feel and absorb that. When you have a terribly toxic roommate, friend, colleague, spouse, or family member, everyone notices it and is negatively affected that it can ruin their day. These emotions that cause others to detect, pick up on, and absorb those other energies off other people is connected to your Clairsentience psychic sense. It acts like a suction cup that breathes in everything that is around it both the good and the bad, the physical and the supernatural and ethereal.

You aura is six feet in all directions around your body. This is how big every human soul's light is. If someone's auric circle is plagued with Darkness and they walk past you, it will hit your auric circle, and this is how it affects you and vice versa. Since everything is made of energy, if you read toxic news that upsets you, the energy of that news and the person that wrote it is emanating off that and hitting your aura. These are all another handful of reasons to protect your Light and sensitivities. This is by getting strict and disciplined by what you allow close to your auric circle. You're doing that to protect you and your soul from unnecessary Dark energies that offer no positive benefit at all.

With Clairsentience you can walk into a place and sense a dark gloom, which is a signal to high tail it out of there. The feelings people have are one of the most powerful ways that psychic information comes in, but when you're so focused on your feelings and how you feel, then you don't realize that sometimes it's actually a psychic hit coming through, until you learn through repetitive practice how to recognize when it is.

It is true that some people tend to display stronger psychic senses than others, but that doesn't mean other people don't have those same psychic senses. The more blocked someone is, then the more reduced those psychic senses are to the extent that it would appear they have no psychic abilities at all.

There is an endless list of things that can block

someone from noticing Divine psychic guidance. The saying that states you are what you eat is true. The foods you consume can create a psychic block with the Divine. The more bad foods you consume, then the dimmer the psychic senses will be. Altering your state of mind through drugs and alcohol will dim your psychic senses. This isn't scolding anyone or instructing anyone not to have those comfort foods like that hot dog at an amusement park or a glass of wine with a lover. This is merely informing you what will diminish your psychic abilities. The good news is that you can have that day of fun where your psychic senses have been dimmed, but then it's assumed it's not like you're doing that everyday. The next day you may then choose to get re-aligned and healthy again. Consuming toxins daily if you're unable to stop should be reduced to moderation beyond enhancing your psychic abilities. It is also less taxing on your body in the long run as your medical doctor may at some point advise you if they haven't already. Believe me I still love my Classic Rock music blaring at a Beach BBQ with a cold beer in my hand, but I know in that moment my psychic prowess is dimming. I can hear my Spirit team council, but they're distant as if talking through a wall.

Negative emotions of any kind will dim those psychic clair senses. This includes any negative emotion you can possibly think of from anger, stress, depression, sadness, grief, agitation, frustration, vindictiveness, greed, and gossip and on and on. I know we basically listed most of the generic negative emotional traits that all human beings experience at one time or another, with some displaying those traits more than others. This isn't telling anyone to deny those emotions, because you will feel them just as the highest holy person will in their own way. We are all having a human experience and with that comes those challenging emotions, but that is one of the reasons why we are having a human experience. It is to be able to control those emotions as much as possible through spiritual maturity. You're allowed to have an off day. You can have numerous off days. The more you work on evolving your soul and physical experience, then the easier it gets in moving yourself right back into faith and centered in the Light when you step off balance.

When one is twenty years old they may overreact emotionally to every little thing, but by the time they're forty years old, one hopes through the challenging life experiences thrown at them and through spiritual maturity they have gotten quite good at re-centering themselves after a bad couple of days. Life experiences throw you a hard fisted right to the face. Many human beings will or have experienced a job loss that causes worry, depression, and fear. Human beings have lovers that leave them causing anger, upset, and sadness. Human beings also experience the loss of loved ones, which can produce a heavy grief and sadness. These are all part of the emotions associated with human life. You feel those emotions and you process them on your own time.

Eventually one hopes you reach a point where you grow exhausted from feeling like that and you begin the process of taking steps to alter that. This can be from reaching out to others for assistance, changing your diet, exercising regularly, shunning or walking away from toxic people. You might choose to listen to music, go into nature to hang out, or read self-help books that can motivate you to feel joy and serenity again. You can also do what I do which is to access God and my Spirit team from within and have them empower me all over again by lifting me right back up into warrior mode ready to conquer the world and forge forward fearlessly. I know that I cannot sit around waiting to die or feeling the same negative emotions day after day with no end in sight. I have to rise back up and get back out there.

An ex once said to me, "The great thing that you do is you rarely get angry, but when you do everyone scatters and we all know it's serious and no drill. But you leave and come back fifteen minutes later and you're all smiles and have got over it. You don't hold onto it for any longer. Most people hang onto it forever never letting it go."

I just said, "How dreadful to hold onto that forever."

Many want the rewards without doing the work. This goes for psychic development as well too. Those that have taken an interest in psychic development want the psychic prowess, but will find the development to opening up the psychic senses to be dull work. If you want any reward, then you have to do the work. There is no way around that, but if you want something bad enough, then you will work hard to achieve it through discipline and hard work.

The soul in the human body is psychic, but the physical body is not psychic. Both the spiritual body and the physical body work in tandem with one another while on Earth. You need to work on both to ensure the other is working at optimum levels. When you work on your physical body by being mindful of what you are doing to it, then this simultaneously strengthens the spiritual body, which brings out those psychic senses. Strengthening your spiritual body can simultaneously strengthen your physical body. This is why taking care of both and keeping them at optimum levels is crucial on your overall well-being for a variety of reasons. One is that it gives you stronger psychic Clair sense channels. Another is that it keeps you physically healthy for as long as possible while you are here. This gives you more energy and focus to dive into your passions and life purpose, as well as fun time with loved ones, friends, and family.

Watch what you ingest each day making sure the ratio from healthy to unhealthy shows the healthy being in a higher percentage while allowing yourself the fun you want to do. Physical exercise has been one of the top things that Spirit showed me since childhood. I subconsciously knew that we have to take care of our bodies. Often there's a disconnect between the body and the soul, but while here they need to work in tandem since they both positively feed off of and work for one another. When you're feeling negative emotions, then this affects your physical body, which transfers to affecting your etheric psychic senses.

Physical exercise would not apply to someone that is physically unable to due to a health issue. This is more for those that don't want to out of laziness or procrastination. I've always been into physical fitness. It started at the early age of five teaching myself to ride a bike on my own, which naturally I fell a number of times, then ran into a cactus on another and created a tiny scar that's still there, but eventually I mastered it and got it going and have continued the exercise routines since. I never even looked at it as work, but have always just enjoyed being active. Decades later and my disciplined exercise routine has yet to permanently stop. Even during my heavy alcohol and drug addicted days, I was still managing to incorporate some exercise on certain days. The stronger your body is made through exercise, then the stronger your psychic channel is. One of my Medium friends rides her bike daily in between reading sessions for clients. She'll also treat herself to the occasional beer. You'll note the balance between the working on our physical body through exercise, but allowing yourself that toxin once in awhile if you choose. Having one beer is different than drinking a six pack.

Your emotional state is just as important as your physical body, both of which also work off each other. When you exercise, there has been scientific evidence that it positively improves your emotional state and well-being. You're improving two things at the same time by doing one thing. That one thing is the exercise that kills two birds with one stone by improving your physical health state and simultaneously your emotional and mental state. There might be a day where I fall into a slump, but then I exercise and hop on the bike and hit the beach. When I arrive back home I feel rejuvenated and uplifted. I've walked into the gym moody, but then after almost an hour of listening to music and working on the weight machines I've found all of that has shifted. Suddenly, I walk out smiling with this uplifting joyful feeling like I'm on top of the world. This is because exercise also helps in raising the feel good Dopamine chemicals in the body.

Those two examples included additional tips that raise your vibration level. When you raise your souls vibration, then the more enhanced your psychic channels get. The biking (exercise) on the beach (nature) is a winning combo because you're uniting two elements that help raise your vibration. You're combining exercise with nature. Getting out into a nature setting has many positive benefits on both your spiritual body and emotional body. Nature has been another scientific proven method that has been shown to reduce stress levels in people. How often have you been feeling tense or edgy, but then you walk through a flower garden or a wide open nature space and you can feel the stress just lift off your body. While at the gym you'll notice I was playing music while working out. Music is another element that raises your vibration. People all over the globe listen to music. Music brings the people together through joy and uplifting fun. It inspires others to create, to work, and to continue on.

Exercising in nature while listening to music is a triple whammy! You're incorporating the exercise, nature, and music all at the same time. It's not rocket science to raise your vibration and increase your psychic senses. God didn't make it complicated where you have to take numerous classes, watch endless videos, and pay enormous amounts of money for a lecture or seminar on it. Just get out there and do it.

Many will always list meditation as a way to increase psychic development, but I've never technically meditated and my psychic channels have forever been off the charts. This doesn't mean that meditation doesn't work. It just means I don't personally do it, but I do admire those that have the patience to sit Indian style in meditation for an hour and never move. I think that takes enormous discipline. Some of the friends I have in the spiritual communities are also huge lovers of meditation. If you're great at meditation and that's what you prefer to do, then that will definitely help in awakening your psychic senses. It's the relaxing element that is key here. The more relaxed you are, and the less negative feelings or thoughts plaguing you, then the easier it is to connect with spirit. It's as simple as that or perhaps not so simple if you struggle with relaxing.

If you're struggling with relaxing and removing negative feelings and thoughts, then that will need to be the first step to take care of. It's not going to happen over night. It's a daily process of working to adjust your state of mind. This would include being able to bounce back out of a circumstance that might have upset or bothered you that day. Once you are feeling good, content, and stress free, then that's a great time to psychically connect.

While I don't sit Indian style in nature meditating for an hour, I do frequent nature settings regularly. My way of meditating is strolling through it with my hands outstretched upwards to feel God move through me, around me, and work on my well-being state, which helps me relax. Sometimes I will kick back and plop in an area on the beach and meditate on the ocean and the crashing of the waves, or I'll head to the desert and plop myself on a rock or an area with little to no people to close my eyes and allow whatever needs to come through to do so. Before I write I will close my eyes, take a deep breath in, call in my team, and center myself, but that doesn't take more than anywhere from one to five minutes max. They come in rather quickly, but this also helps in centering myself. I suppose in a sense meditation professionals would say that's all meditating.

Sometimes we get busy and distracted by the day to day practical parts of our lives, which is understandable, but then the Divine messages get lost during that time. Spirit will do their best to make the messages as known as they possibly can. Sometimes it's subtle, but other times it's so obvious that you can't miss it.

All souls have built in psychic clair senses within them that allow spirit messages to flow into sometimes without you realizing it. The four main psychic clair senses that I've mentioned throughout this book are Clairvoyance, Clairsentience, Claircognizance and Clairaudience.

Clairvoyance means clear viewing, which is the psychic information is projected to you through your Third Eye in between your physical eyes. Clairsentience means clear sensing, which is the psychic information comes through the feelings you get. If I feel a physical ailment on myself, it sometimes ends up being someone around me that has that physical ailment. This is an example of a Clairsentience psychic hit. Claircognizance means clear knowing, which is the psychic information coming through your sense of knowing. This would be where you just know something is going to happen or you know the information without having been versed in it. Clairaudience means clear hearing, which is the psychic information comes through an etheric voice speaking it. Anything that comes through those psychic senses would be something that ends up coming true. That would be the obvious key that it was a psychic hit and not your ego or the Darkness messing with you. Every thought or feeling someone has is not a psychic hit or a mediumship dialogue from Spirit. More often than not it's the mindless chatter of the ego. This is why being especially cognizant of what's going on in and around you can help you differentiate what is coming through is you, the ego, and lower self, as opposed to it being Divine psychic information or your higher self.

PROTECT YOUR LIGHT

It's never been unusual for me to foresee upcoming events, but I've never looked at that as psychic fortune telling. I looked at it as an extension of me and what my Spirit team council were choosing to communicate to me. More often than not their communication flushes in an automatic random way. I can be busy doing other things, then a psychic alert flies in indicating something is about to take place. Other times it's something insignificant where I'm walking and clairvoyantly see a woman in green jogging. Ten minutes later a woman in green appears jogging down the sidewalk past me and that's the end of that. There's no reason for that foresight.

In the film *The Silence of the Lambs*, there is a scene where Clarice Starling (Jodie Foster) is communicating to Hannibal Lecter (Anthony Hopkins) through his cell. In the middle of their conversation his head lifts up as if sensing something, then he looks back down glaring at her, "Dr. Chilton I presume. I believe you two know each other."

She stares at him strangely not understanding, then a beat later Dr. Chilton shows up with the authorities to escort her out of the building. In that subtle movement, that audience members might've missed, it would be interpreted it that he psychically sensed Dr. Chilton was on his way. This is because there were no audible sounds of him being close and nor was he in physical view.

One of my many psychic light protection devices is to not engage with negative people or negative spirits for that matter, which should be observed whether or not one is a sensitive psychic being. This is something I've adopted early on in my life as a teenager, but accelerated that mantra during my twenties growing more strict about it. It also makes it challenging or frustrating for some people to get close to me right away unless they work for it. This is because I've always been doubly cautious about anyone I don't know that approaches me. I typically take a step back to observe and read them to see if they are safe enough or not. I can immediately tell if someone is bathed in darkness, lower energy, or has any measure of an ulterior motive. Part of this is due to who is getting too close to my Light that it affects me physically. I need to govern my vessel with the most ultimate protection possible, because that comes first. The other reason is due to my distrust in others due to the childhood abuse and the failed relationships that followed and broke apart due to the other partner's lack of integrity.

Combine both of those reasoning's for keeping people at arms length and you have a supremely difficult person on your hands whose got a wall around him the size of China. This doesn't mean it's impossible, since I'm surrounded by people that have been around for years and decades. This means they were able to scale that wall, so it's not impossible for the strong and trustworthy. This goes both ways since those in my circles have told others that I'm one of the strongest and trustworthy people they know. You treat people how you want to be treated. It's been conveyed I'm strong and trustworthy and they mirror that right back at me, thus a beautiful long-term connection is created.

There are occasions where a negative person, spirit, or spirits can and will get into your aura and infect your light. Sometimes you can be doing everything right and it still gets on in there. It can cause all sorts of anxiety, turmoil, and a domino effect of back to back negative things happening in your life. It's just not worth the risk to invite in anyone that you suspect is infected, or that you psychically pick up on as having a lower energy. This is part of protecting your light, since your guides can only do so much. They'll warn you through your psychic senses and you can choose to ignore that warning or follow it. Many have admitted to ignoring it, then later when a multitude of negative circumstances hits the fan regarding the person, they will later say, "I knew something was off with that person when I met them, but I ignored it."

CHAPTER THIRTEEN

Psychically Connecting

and Other Psychic Wisdom

The higher degree of psychic connectivity, then the higher degree of sensitivities, anxiety, and insomnia you may have. This doesn't mean this is the case with every single person, but for the most part it tends to be the trend. The reason is that a great deal of the ethereal interruptions that take place on the psychic system can cause the side effects of the anxiety and insomnia. When you have a high degree of psychic sensitivity, then walking out into a crowd is challenging because the likelihood of absorbing or sensing some kind of erratic energy will be high. No matter how disciplined a person like this is, no matter how many prayers, shielding, and meditations you do, it is still near impossible to prevent these sorts of psychic stimuli from entering the soul's shield.

Due to the hyper mental and emotional activity and the psychic interference attempting to make its way into my world every second makes life more challenging. It has a tendency to keep me on high alert all night, on and off through the night, or it will yank me awake and on guard. I've had to get up and pace or open the windows to shake it off. This lifelong insomnia was noticed early on in childhood where I'd be laying up in bed all night or abruptly ripped out of sleep.

When particular planetary aspects are especially intense, then this increases this activity. The insomnia grows worse and I'm forced to detach and lay low as much as possible. It's been bad enough that I have talked to doctors about it. My Spirit team eventually showed me the connection between what I was experiencing physically and the psychic activity. I was aware of both, how I was feeling physically, and the psychic hits I'd receive, but it took awhile before they pointed out that they were connected to each other.

This isn't the case every single time since you will need to put on the psychic detective hat to decipher if what you're experiencing is psychic activity coming through or not.

The following list is an example of some of the things that can explain away the reasons for repetitive anxiety, insomnia, and other negative emotions before you can come to the conclusion that it is psychic activity:

• You received some bad news that day or recently pertaining to your life or someone close to you. This could include things like the loss of a job, relationship breakup, passing of a loved one, legal issues, you have to give a speech/perform, any kind of personal or professional life issue can cause it, etc.

• Examine the foods you've been eating since that will have an effect on your system.

• Did you drink alcohol, smoke/ingest weed, or take any kind of drug that alters your perception.

• Look at the pills or supplements you take each day or might have taken the day you experienced the unexplainable activity.

• Talk to a Doctor to rule out any kind of medical condition or issue going on.

When you've ruled out every possible physical reason, then it could be there is psychic activity and paranormal interference coming in. The activity seems to increase at night because you're not distracted by the day to day practical world. You're alone, quiet, and motionless with your thoughts.

When the psychic activity or challenging planetary aspects rear its ugly head, then everything in my life comes to a complete stand still during that time, no writing done, nothing. Most meetings and appointments get cancelled. My strict exercise regimen gets hit, which is unusual since I'll exercise and work out even if I'm dead. If I'm too out of it due to the lack of sleep, then I'm basically useless. I can write easy personal emails and make friend phone calls since they don't care what state I'm in and understand my nature. Other than that I use that time to lay low and hang out in nature. I will sometimes lie down in a nature setting and allow the nature spirits energy to envelop and heal me.

During those heavy anxiety moments I also end up on high alert. The fun part or not so fun part is the insomnia gets out of control. Eyes wide open vigilant like an animal. That part is tough because too much psychic overload is flying in at once. When certain testy planetary energy is in motion, I can feel that friction without knowing there is a tough transit going on. Every single time this happens, I'm never surprised to find it's an unstable planetary time. There isn't anything I can do to make it stop as the energy pull is too strong. I just have to ride it out and wait for the storm to pass, and it will lighten up because as it is said...this too shall pass.

No spirit writing or work involving my mental aptitude takes place during those times. That is temporarily closed for refurbishment throughout the days of little sleep. It's different than the regular bouts of spiritual maintenance I do every so often the way you take your car in for maintenance.

When anything is especially intense, it's best to be patient and ride it out as much as possible. There have been the rare times when my insomnia goes on for several consecutive nights. I'm laying up all night going mentally crazy and frustrated. I need my disciplined nightly eight hours of sleep to function at optimum levels. I know that I cannot continue one more night like that.

As the sun sets on day four of bad sleep and the darkness comes upon me, I mumble with the horrid anxiety to God and my Spirit team, "Please let me sleep tonight, please, please, please. You have to help. I cannot do this one more night. I can't. Bring everybody in if you have to."

And thank God I finally sleep that night. The despair is vastly great at that point that Divine intervention finally comes through. The sound sleep feels so good that I'm stunned because it feels like being saved.

Once I sleep fully through the night again, then I'm back to peak levels physically and spiritually. The spirit communication starts flooding in effortlessly and clearly upon waking, then I spend that day catching up on the writing work for any days lost.

It can be strange during that period when spirit communication is quieter, but as soon as I fully sleep it is like the door slams open and the Light floods in again. The second my eyes open after the first nights sleep, then the channel is fully open and in movement. I smile and say, "Thank you, God! I'm back. Rejoice!"

Some measure of good sound sleep is essential to psychically and divinely connect on a deeper level since the physical health is connected to psychic health.

INVITING IN SPIRIT TO BE PART OF THE TEAM

I typically feel the strongest jolt when the Holy Ghost moves through me. Those moments are definitely memorable because it's that connection which produces uplifting love, joy, and serenity. I'm not someone known for shedding tears that easily, so when I do in this case it's to illustrate how powerful it is that it shakes me to the core.

Swiftly detach from ego in order to move into the face of Spirit and back out again as needed. It is also how one learns to tame the beast of the darkness of ego

Calling in my Spirit team, I don't typically conduct any special ceremonies, even though I have friends in the community that do. Everyone has their own ways of doing things they prefer. My method has always been on the simpler side, where I just plain ask a guide or angel to come in for me the way I would ask anyone for something.

For example, there was a period in my life where my union with Archangel Michael was growing stronger over time. It wasn't like day one the request for him to be my personal body-soul guard happened and it was done. He was coming in sporadically at first. As time went on my relationship bond with him grew stronger that it became permanent on its own.

At one point we had the conversation where we made this united pact that he would be there permanently. Part of that was also because I get distracted with Earthly life situations and things would happen. If he was already next to me full time, then it was just easier for all of us to have him be part of the team. And also he wanted to the way God wants a relationship with His children.

There was a point when I made a firm request with Archangel Michael. I invited him in permanently through an invitation that was real the way you would commit to a love partner. You want this, they want this, and it is done. It's also similar to what Christ followers mean when they say, "Have you asked Jesus to come into your heart?"

Some people don't know what that means, but it's similar to my relationship with Archangel Michael. He becomes a part of you as Jesus Christ is a part of me as well too. I love Christ's goodness, compassion, and forgiveness. He also helps me stay centered amidst an inner and outer world of chaos.

With Archangel Michael, this is the same way you meet someone new who is going to end up being one of your close friends. It's not like you're instantly best friends on the first day - at least not in my life. It's over time as you're both showing up for the relationship does it start to grow stronger. This was the same way it was with Archangel Michael. It was allowing him in on occasion. I was thinking okay, let me see what you can do and why do you want to be here? I'd try him on like a pair of jeans that I'd wear once in awhile, until I started to wear them everyday by spending more time with him, then the relationship bond started to grow. This concept is similar with all I've connected with whether in spirit or in people. It's the same way someone develops any relationship that grows stronger over time. It's spending more time with them and developing a legitimate loyal relationship with them. Now he's just part of the air I breathe that I can't imagine him not being around anymore. I'm too used to his presence and him being around for so long. I would know if he ever left, but he hasn't. I don't think twice about it. I wake up and he's already there even if I'm not coherent yet.

CONNECTING WITH SPIRIT

Some psychics or mediums meditate to get into a trance like state. The reason this is an effective method for them is because you're taking at least a few minutes to quiet your mind. You're silencing everything around you in order to have a stronger connection with the other side. When you quiet your thoughts and the noise of the outside world, then there is room for Spirit and God to come rushing in. Silencing everything is by removing any traces of negativity from your aura. If you're upset about something, then this will make it difficult to channel or connect until you let that go and release it. It's best to wait until you're in a relaxed state, even if that means pushing the psychic or medium session to another day.

When you've moved into a state of reception, then the messages and guidance from above flows into your soul through one of your psychic clair sense channels and the connection is made. The first step to getting closer to channeling naturally is by being aware of your own soul and what's outside of it. When you pay attention and notice all of the physical distracting noises, then you're able to diminish those sounds. You can do that when you're out and about in a busy area such as a street or at a mall.

Some of the ways of fine tuning your clear hearing Clairaudience psychic sense channel would include listening to sounds that are typically grating on a sensitive person. For the purpose of understanding the distinctive differences between the psychic channel and physical channel it's helpful to do it for a few minutes.

Perk up your ears hearing the noisy symphonic physical sounds coming from the rumbling of cars, tires skidding, garbage cans banging, sirens going off, people talking or shouting, and so on. Notice the distracting energy on your phone and the things you aim your focus towards while on it. The key is being aware when it has become a distraction. Once you're able to notice these differences, you not only realize how distracted the planet is, but you're then able to work on dissolving those sounds from your mind to tune it out. When it is tuned out, the noise level of spirit begins to rise.

Spirit is already loud, but when it sounds as if they're non-existent, far away, or muted, it is because you're either blocked, or the sounds of the physical part of the world are turned up way too high around you. Those sounds include the noise of your own thoughts. It's like you're blasting your music at home while you and a guest are trying to talk over it. You keep saying, "What?" You then turn the music down a little in order to hear one another. Turning the physical distractions down enables one to hear the voice of Heaven clearer. I've been driving with my music blaring while simultaneously communicating with Spirit effortlessly because their words travel over the chords of music for me. The downfall is I'm blasting the music. There have been times that I'm asking them what they said telepathically. I'd say, "Say that again." They'd finally shout, "Turn it down!" I'm thrown off reaching to turn my own stereo down, then I can hear them clearly.

Psychic Accuracy

If a Claircognizance thought or Clairsentient sense feeling hit comes true, then it's obvious to note that the thoughts and feelings were real and not coming from the ego. You can get better at discerning what is an ominous premonition to an ego thought the more you use those Clair senses. Being hyper self-aware of everything within and around your entire world helps. If repeated dark thoughts plague your mind, then examine your current well-being state. If one week you're suffering from raised depression or anxiety feelings, then the ominous thoughts can be ego based. You would need to rule other possibilities out such as what's going on in your physical life that could be causing it. Examine what foods, drinks, and supplements you're ingesting as that has an effect as well too. If you're on cloud nine and everything is great, then you get a random rush of something negative, but it doesn't knock your current happy state of mind off balance, then it could likely be a psychic premonition.

A premonition typically continues to come into your consciousness repeatedly. Whereas ego thoughts are all over the place, fear based, and inconsistent. If it's a death feeling, it doesn't necessarily mean an actual death is going to happen. More likely than not, it is that there could be a circumstance coming that might be challenging, either with you or someone around you. It can be a metaphysical death or the ending of one way of life. It can also indicate a major soul life transformation is about to take place. It depends on numerous factors that include what the thought or feeling is, what and where your state of mind is at during the time of the thought or feeling, as well as other circumstances going on around you that could play a part.

The majority of fear based thoughts tend to turn out to be untrue. This is especially when someone is over worrying about something that ends up working out the way it's supposed to. It's more than accepting or receiving the feeling or thought. It's paying attention to you and your surroundings to gauge how the information, guidance, and messages are coming into your senses, and at what frequency you're operating at on that particular day. This all requires a hyper alertness and extreme discipline with ones life and lifestyle. It takes constant daily work to become a strong healthy psychic vessel. You cannot do it one week, then get lazy a week later and then try to do it again two months later. You're basically starting all over when you put it off, so it is necessary to work at it. It's like taking certain vitamins or supplements where you have to take them regularly to notice the positive benefits over time.

When it comes to beginning psychic development, many have informed me that they feel like they're making something up until the person they relayed the information to informs them that it was true. One key trait to remember is to trust. Trust what you're getting and don't worry if you're going to be wrong since that's a given. The information may not mean anything to you, but it may mean something to someone. The other thing is to not worry if you make a mistake or get something wrong. There's no reason to say, "This may be wrong, but I'm getting that..."

People already know you may be wrong or it ends up not being true. There's no need to say that. The only times I've said something remotely close to that is when someone is upset by what I'm seeing, then I may say something like, "I hope I'm wrong for your sake."

Unfortunately, due to them being used to my accuracies, they fear that it is unlikely to be inaccurate.

Clairvoyant hits will sometimes be brought to you through your dreams. It's your soul's job to decode the messages in your dreams. Jot down what happened in the dream before you forget it, then break up everything that was happening in the dream that you can remember and juxtapose this with what you're going through in your daily life at that time. It's a puzzle to put together to decipher what's being relayed to you from above. You could be getting a symbol or sign about something, but often psychic information is not exactly coming in the way one might think it means. You could get a symbol of a car, which might make one think they're going to buy a new car, but it can also be a road trip, an accident, or something else entirely with a car being the psychic clue. Sometimes there is no point or message in a dream. It's your subconscious projecting those images to you, while other times it is a Divine message.

There are people that can see this if they have strong Clairvoyance, but even if they don't they may see these things while in a lucid dreaming state. This is because the main part of your conscious is asleep, which helps in removing those lower self sabotaging blocks that would prevent you from seeing it while in a waking state. Those things some see that are similar to one another are real, but just in another plane seeping into this plane.

When you deliver spirit information to another person, keep in mind of what Heaven's set of guidelines are. They include that you only state what you're being told by them to others in a way that is objective and compassionate. Say what you see, sense, know or hear, but avoid instructing the person what to do. Only go as far as to say, "If you do this, then this is what will happen."

If the other person says, "Which one should I do?"

The response should be, "That's up to you to decide." Your best friends or family might tell you what to do, but when you go to an objective psychic reader, then they should remain neutral. This includes never telling someone that their death, or someone close to them, is imminent.

Another psychic rule of etiquette is avoid entering someone's aura and giving them information unless they've expressed permission. Not doing that is similar to breaking into someone's house, which is an invasion of privacy. Especially don't do that to relay negative information. I heard one person that wasn't a practicing psychic telling people things like when their death is going to be, or not to drive because they're going to be getting into a major accident some day, and that there is a major Earthquake going to happen any day now. Basically as many bad things as you can think of, this person was randomly telling people that. The people he was telling this to never asked him, it was randomly volunteered, and nor was he accurate anyway. The ego wants a new person to believe they're super psychic all of a sudden. This prompts them to runaround making outlandish uncalled for statements, which screams of inexperience and gives practicing or professional psychics a bad name.

An exception to this rule would be if you're friends with this person and you randomly blurt out things not realizing you're making a psychic statement. I've never personally blurted out something considered tragic like their death or a car accident. I keep those negative things to myself. I'm always moving cautiously and would never interrupt someone to say something off like, "I need to warn you, there is an airplane that's going to be hurled at your head next week. Avoid sitting on your living room couch."

Contrary to some Hollywood films, most psychic information that comes in are not big loud tragedies. The giveaway would be the person seems to recite that to everybody on top of not being asked permission for it.

Part of mediumship and psychic etiquette is that you are responsible when it comes to how you word or deliver information as much as possible. This also includes deciding whether or not it's your place to offer information. I've had some email me or my Editor to say that my Spirit Guides are trying to get my attention regarding an issue, so my guides are going through that person to tell me. My Editor said he's told people, "If his Spirit Guides are trying to relay a message to him, believe me he has no problem retrieving it on his own."

Approaching random people or messaging those you don't know to relay things like that is inappropriate human behavior, but it's also poor psychic etiquette. If you're bent on relaying psychic information, then ask the person if it would be okay if you psychically read them. If they say no they don't want you entering their auric energy field, then move on. If they say yes, then carry on with the reading.

PSYCHIC TIMING

One of the soul lessons that all have is to learn patience. Spirit isn't handing blessings to you immediately as soon as you ask for it. They're not always going to relay psychic information on you if they know it isn't Divine timing for it yet. If you knew everything that was going to happen to you, then you would no longer live life. You might sit back, relax, and wait for the date that something is supposed to happen. Not doing anything is an action step. You are choosing not to do anything, which will block the circumstance from happening while altering your souls path. This is because you stopped doing anything and think, "This will land on my lap anyway, so I may as well do nothing."

If everyone was being handed stuff right away, then no one would learn anything. When I was sixteen years old, I knew I was going to work in the film business, but I didn't know when. Spirit showed me visuals of me in there and in that world. I knew it was coming, but I had no idea when exactly. All I knew was that it was on its way to happen fairly soon. At the age of twenty-three, I received that call that changed my life and got me into the film business with one of the top five bankable movie stars at the time. This was seven years after the original psychic hits that were showing me in that world. The predicted psychic forecast eventually happened, but not as quickly as I thought. If my Spirit team said I'd get it in three months and it didn't happen, then I'd be disappointed and let down, or I wouldn't have done anything to help move it along.

When you push for something to happen, then that pushes it further away. That impulsive energy creates a block that delays it from happening.

Psychic timing is often impossible to predict, because there are numerous factors to consider that would delay something from taking place. It is true there have been occasions where I have predicted timing to the exact day. One thing to note is those were rare times when Spirit did give me a date and it happened on that date because no parties involved were delaying it through free will actions. Spirit doesn't usually offer exact timing in many cases. They might just say soon or further out in the distance.

If I receive timing, then I'll say it out loud, but if I don't get any timing, then that just means I'm not being given timing for whatever reason. Sometimes forecasted predictions of what's to come are given by spirit on a need to know basis. There are times that even your Spirit team doesn't have the psychic answer to your question, because it is being blocked by God for them too. If it's blocked for them, then it's blocked for you. If they are exempt from knowing when something is to take place themselves, then they won't give timing. If they know when it'll happen, they will only say it if it has any benefit for the particular person. Perhaps the person has been waiting for years and has become discouraged to the point they've stopped trying and given up on life. In that case, if Spirit has the answer, then they will offer reassurance to the person that the event is indeed in the soul's contract to take place and to keep on believing, have faith, and remain patient. This is why sometimes you might have seen or heard others about to give up, but then a sliver of light shines in revealing some light blessings on the horizon, then this shakes that soul out of its rut motivating them to keep going.

This is not always the case, because sometimes God and Spirit need the human being to do their part. Many spend each day complaining that nothing good ever comes to help them. They lack motivation, passion, and drive. As a result, they ensure this state continues and so does God. Spirit is not about dropping blessings onto a soul that is stuck in sloth mode if the soul won't get up to put in somewhat of an effort. Putting in any effort repetitively prompts God to swoop in and start lighting more of the way. If you are paralyzed by fear, sadness, or any other negative emotion, then pray for help with that element first.

Other general reasons timing isn't given also are that there are still circumstances that need to take place that will enlighten that person some more before what they want arrives. If it comes too soon before someone is ready, then it'll slip through that person's fingers because they weren't in a position to accept it in the right spirit, even if they think they are. What your ego believes and what God sees are two separate things.

Spirit is doing their best to make it happen, but there are pieces within the puzzle that need to be maneuvered to orchestrate the circumstance to happen. It could be that Spirit is making it happen, such as they are bringing a certain soul mate person to you, but you both keep missing each other. One of you is not noticing the other one or you keep ignoring them. Neither of you are acting on it every time Spirit gets you in the room together.

Timing is fluid and non-existent in the spirit world.

They have no concept of time because they don't operate on human made clocks. Timing is something human beings created because they function according to a clock. Timing is a foreign language to Spirit, even though they are aware we are operating by a clock created by us, but they don't care if their timing is not the same as your timing. We see things as a matter of racing against the clock, but they see it as an unimportant blip.

What if someone gives another person timing in a reading? What if that time frame predicted comes and nothing transpires as expected? One might assume the reader was off, wrong, or was being nice to try and give an estimated guess to satisfy the client. I've heard those stories, but then a year later the prediction comes true. Events took place that shifted the timing because Spirit cannot control the free will actions of human beings. They're not going to freely give timing to any reader, because Spirit doesn't care about the ego dramatics that human beings have where we want something now. They don't care about the ego's angry frustrated irritation. They will instead urge you to learn the lesson of patience.

CHAPTER FOURTEEN

Stay Centered Psychic Warrior

There was one particular moment in my life when I had consumed so many pills that I ended up throwing them up not long afterwards. The pills did not have a chance to dissolve or be completely absorbed into my physical system before Divine intervention entered the picture.

Minutes after taking the pills, I psychically sensed a rumbling in the room around me. My third eye slammed open revealing a doorway into an open field bathed in bright light. Before I discovered what was going on, the presence of God Himself morphed into a fist flying towards me at rapid speed like a snake coming in for an attack, but this was the energy of a concerned Father. His hand glided purposefully towards me that it caused my breath to accelerate in dread and my heart rate to go up. God's fisted hand soared at great speed with no sign of stopping that it caused me to inhale in shock with my mouth open wide enough for his fist to soar right down into it, down my throat, and into my stomach. His hand fished around grabbing all of the pills then His hand glided back the other way yanking them all out of me like an exorcism.

I could feel His hand flying through my throat and yanking them all out. It hit me out of nowhere like being sucker punched in the gut. As I coughed and threw up the un-dissolved pills, I heard a few members of my Spirit team council on the Other Side in unison calmly come forward to say with nonchalance as if it was no big deal, "We're getting all of this out of you. You don't need it."

It felt like my body went through a panting workout as if I had just come back from one of my long jogs outside. My Clairvoyance opened up even wider and my Claircognizance psychic sense blasted open into a massive beautiful awakened state that brought this warrior back to top form again. Struggling to find eternal centered balance between this world and the next has cause immeasurable suffering on my mental health state that fluctuates up and down throughout each day. This is what it's like when your soul is a heightened psychic sponge absorbing all of the good and bad around you every second. You don't get to wake up one morning and say, "I'll take the day off from psychically absorbing anything."

The main self, the top dog consciousness, the leader that runs the show protecting all detached and dissociated separated selves within me that broke apart due to those prison years of traumatic child abuse, fought through my broken body. Eyes faced forward with crystal clear focused euphoria hunching back down into a frozen state, as the highest self warrior took center stage again gleaming angrily and into that infamous cold Wise One annoyance, "You had no right to stop me."

The Divine illumination offered by God was that my rebellious statement was a false one. They did have a right to stop me, since I originally gave them permission to intervene in my life prior to that moment ages ago when needed. I gave them 100% full consent any time or place to make this Heavenly request immensely impermeable that even I cannot break it no matter how strong my force of will is. Force of will and determination is something granted at my soul's conception. When God made me He knew this particular soul would be one of His warriors. This is just as your soul was carefully made with love and pure intention and a reason for existing.

No spirit being can interfere with your free will choice unless you give them expressed permission. The exceptions would include a life threatening obstruction that could potentially result in death before the time your soul is contracted to exit this plane. In my case, had I not asked for 100% consented spiritual intervention, they still could have stepped in to do what they can to prevent my premature death, since it is not my time to cross back through the veil and head back home yet. As human history has shown, not all guides and angels have been successful at stopping premature deaths, but there is only so much they can do. Like human beings, they too run into roadblocks, which are namely us and our free will and resistance to staying centered in the Light during those moments our human physical flesh experience gets in the way.

When I stuffed my temporary body with pills, I wasn't depressed or trying to kill myself since suicide is not something that crosses my mind, but as an over sensitive psychic vessel that pulsates and fluctuates with the tiniest brush, I experience the depths of pain that the suicidal feel. Most of the time it isn't my pain, but those whose presence is close enough to the auric field around my physical body. It can be too much to withstand in this Earthly sphere.

I grew obsessed with numbing and dulling the pain associated with the toxins my soul absorbed and absorbs from the child abuse, to the neurosis that exist in the different selves within me, to the psychic stimuli that never shuts off, to the naïve human souls on the planet. There are times that I cannot take it anymore and need to shut it off. Since it never shuts off even if I ask it too, I have weakened and succumbed to doing what I can to shut it off, even if that means through artificial methods. In my late teens to early twenties, this was through cigarettes to calm the anxiety riddled rage and pain associated with the repetitive abuse, which eventually led to alcohol dependence where I'd sometimes keep drinking until I'd black out or wake up in my own vomit. The next step on that evolution of compulsions was naturally drugs.

During my drug addicted days, I would do a line of cocaine, but then drink carrot juice right after that, as if that would cancel it out. This depiction is to illustrate the opposing dichotomies between me reasoning away doing something bad, but mixing it with something good to balance it. This was my ego mind justifying what I was doing with God and my Spirit team who I had been acquainted with since my toddler years. I knew through them what I was doing would cause more pain, but they were dealing with a human child that was dealing with immeasurable suffering on his own. And like many young people, my rebelliousness was out of control and off the charts, including with God and my Spirit team. Luckily, in time with their help I was able to clean up my toxic behavior like the drugs, the large amounts of alcohol, and the cigarettes. They helped me get on a cleaner healthier path by the time I was moving through my twenties. The drugs were done by twenty-three, and the cigarettes and my alcohol addiction was cleaned up by the time I was twenty-six. This was replaced by full on body, mind, spirit exercises that increased and became more disciplined and warrior like as I grew older.

Our bodies should be looked up on as shrines you take care of with the greatest precision and care. Often there's a disconnect or a separation between the physical body and the soul. They both enhance one another pending they are being equally attended to. This wouldn't apply to someone physically unable to due to a health issue.

When it comes to psychic phenomena, people will either believe in it, they might be open to the possibility, or they flat out refuse to believe in such "nonsense", as they might say to voice their disapproval. As God and my Spirit team council have informed me time and again, they don't care if people don't believe it. The ones that do believe in it may glorify it as if it's something cool to be psychic or develop ones psychic gifts. It's not entertainment sensing every single shred of heightened nuance each second. Battling with the lifelong anxiety that comes with the stronger sixth sense is both a gift and a curse. The gift is those are the receptors I use to connect with Spirit and the Divine to help make sounder choices in life, but not for the sole sake of predicting the future. The heightened psychic foresight to what's coming is a side effect to the blessing.

This is one of the reasons it's nearly impossible for me to be in crowds unless necessary or if I have no choice. I've turned down invites to functions and events for the reasons of not being emotionally ready. Some automatically assume anyone like that is a snob or conceited, but it's much deeper than that. This is not a planet known for its depth as a twenty year old reader eloquently said to me once. I pondered his deeper words that would typically come from someone of older age, or in this case I was dealing with an old soul. If this planet was known for depth, then there would be no crime, suffering, anger, hatred, depression, anxiety, sadness, vindictiveness, and on and on. Spirit knows how exhausting it must be to live in those well-being states.

On the one hand it's understood that some people are either born this lifetime with a challenging mental health disposition, or it's developed over time as it was in my case at the hands of one of my caregivers that was supposed to love and protect, not incite harm and permanent psychological damage. For others they choose to reside in those negative states when they have the strength of will inside them to pull themselves out of that state. You can choose not to read your Twitter feed or gossip media that's filled with negativity. You can choose not to engage with someone that you know will only get a dramatic rise out of you. Deep down many desire happiness, but it seems to be a chore to get happy.

You're likely open to concepts like psychic phenomena and soul growth, although there are those that will dive into something knowing they won't like it. You've noticed that in those instances where someone attacks an artist or entertainer they hate, even though that was their original assessment before going in. Corrupted egos tend to focus on the negative and will seek out things they hate rather than things that bring them joy. It that respect, they have a choice to choose to partake in activities they enjoy, or they can choose to follow the misery.

Many human souls hang out on the surface of superficiality unable to penetrate its attractive sphere. The few that manage to get their feet wet in the darkest depths grow confused and lost. I know what it's all like, as I too partially functioned on the superficial more often than not during my artificial years of the late teens and early twenties, but with the Divine's guidance I rapidly evolved out of that. I realized then that I hadn't found what I was looking for. I had one part of me that was superficial, but the other part that was stronger and could easily access deep spiritual psychic information without trying since birth. It was this tug of war between my soul spirit and the physical flesh.

All soul beings have layers of complexity underneath. The superficial have the capacity to reach those depths when they do the work that helps them evolve. They continuously educate themselves, do the research and the work, while maintaining an open mind. The world is too rigid and one-sided in its human viewpoints of what they like or don't like that there is no room for anything different. Perception is limited to what you were trained to focus on growing up. If you grew up on an unhealthy diet of trash television, reality television, gossip, time wasting apps, and technological devices, then growth is stunted and stalled until you break through that monotony to realize there has to be more than this.

Absorbing the energies being darted at me everyday is challenging on my equilibrium. The other sensitive beings that understand this know of the turmoil and aggravation it can cause in your life. Trapped in this temporary human body can be too much to take all of that external energy in. It takes effort and work every second you breathe to navigate through life and enjoy it while simultaneously being this huge psychic sponge absorbing everything around you. You adopt a strict disciplined set of rules that assists in making physical human circumstances tolerable.

These are rules such as you watch what you ingest into your body, even when your sensitivities are bouncing off the charts prompting you to dull it down with anything you can get your hands onto. It's taking care of yourself on all levels through exercise, frequent visits to a nature setting, whether it is a park or your own backyard. It's cleaning up your diet as much as possible and focusing on balancing that with fruits and vegetables. Foods that existed before human kind began tampering with it and putting chemicals and hormones into it. Even though it's perfectly okay to have some fun and have those comfort foods. This is about incorporating more balance into your world, which can positively or negatively affect your mental health and well-being psychic state.

Earthly life is tough for more people than not, but it is especially tough on the sensitive souls. It is the ultra-sensitive that psychically see, feel, know, and hear more than the average soul. It can be challenging to stay centered in a world that doesn't believe in that, understand it, or care for that matter. This is a clue that you came here for a reason, even if that reason is to shine that bright light of love that is your basic nature to all you encounter.

CHAPTER FIFTEEN

Bend To No Wind

Psychic Warrior

Through various connections with my team, they have forever shown me as a warrior hunter on the Other Side and that my name is *Zayin* back home, which in ancient text means "sword", "to arm", or "sword to arm". The irony are the parallels of them showing me as a warrior hunter in endless visions on the other side and then one day began telling me what my name really is on the Other Side. From that point forward it never stopped coming in.

I remember when it first came in as I was in the California desert alone surrounded by the impressively ferocious warm winds where Spirits communication comes in powerfully strong. Divine spirit messages also travel over the atoms and particles of oxygen. The cleaner and clearer the air quality, then the easier those messages and guidance can come through. My hyper alertness was in top form as I opened my mouth thinking, "That's my name?" It continued to come in rolling off my telepathic tongue that wasn't moving leaving me mesmerized as if coming to a grand realization. There isn't one person that wouldn't want to meet their real selves and know who their soul truly is. The experience is indescribable filling in all of the blanks the way it might be for an adopted child to discover who their birth parents are. Through your own psychic experiences and visions you'll be shown who you are on Divine timing, because every soul has a home base tribe back home in Heaven.

The endless psychic foresight they've continuously poured through my visions and consciousness to remind me of who I am was for the sake of keeping the faith. It was to continuously remind me not to give up on my purpose or goals because there is a grander reason for it even when I don't feel like doing something or I want to quit. I'm reminded I can't quit. That's not in my soul's warrior DNA.

All souls have a name they are known by back home in Heaven. The name you have as a human being were names your parent or guardian gave you when you were born and that was your temporary identity for this one Earthly lifetime. Deep down at the core of your soul you know your soul's truer identity that transcends time and space beyond this plane. You know who you are when you arrive back home. Everyone on Earth is travelling through this passing reality is all. The older you age on Earth, the more you know that you're closer to going back home than you've ever been. Looking at it as being almost home rather than almost dead has a much more prolific impacting ring to it.

The lifelong battle with demons in my personal life is always matched with the others from beyond the veil consistently pointing me towards the Light. As one of God's warriors, when that soul part of me rose up in this life in the body I currently inhabit, he broke through the wall with his fist so hard it caused Hell to rattle uncomfortably.

Visualize what a warrior soldier's job entails. A warrior is trained to be strong enough to withstand all forms of battle in the face of adversity. This carries over to all aspects of the warrior's life. The warrior is prompted to go to battle quite a bit! The warrior may be weary from battle, yet they stand strong, stoic, and at attention like an exceptional General never faltering. They can be difficult to be with if around the wrong type of person, but they tend to be surrounded by an equally strong loyal circle they consider to be on the same level. They don't work for someone, they work with.

My Wise One warrior rage and ferocious strength comes out once in awhile. One of my friends was recalling me bothered about something that was coming to fruition. He said I paced back and forth, then called out growling in perfect preacher-y, "God, come on, I need you man! I've shown up for you, now you show up for me!"

There is no messing around when it comes to my faith and spiritual connections. Be happy that God is blessing other people over you, but it's okay to say, "I'm glad you're blessing them, and by the way I'm in that line too!"

I've often asked, "How do you know a decision is right?"

I've pointed upwards towards God, "I already know."

With the Boxing Sport, feeling the confidence is one of the most important elements of entering a match. It is feeling it inside and knowing that you're going to win. When you go to a match knowing that you're going to win that match, the odds are you're going to win that match. This is the same concept in how a Warrior of Light is trained to perceive anything and everything. Imagine consistently having the stance of being primed for battle even when there is no reason to be. You cannot help it, because it's in your DNA. A warrior will personally never change it for anything in the world even if the entire universe was against them. Dive into your life purpose, your pursuits, and your activism knowing you will win.

Every decision you make is like getting dressed spiritually. You put on the armor of God. Put on the shield of the Light's justice. This is by standing in the compassion of God and walking in faith. Become who your soul truly is. When you wear the spiritual armor, then this helps protect you from the darkness of the enemy. It helps you stay centered in peace in order to strengthen your connection. Whenever I begin each day, I will get spiritually dressed. This is more than looking good on the exterior, since I don't care all that much about that. I'm a jeans and flip-flops mostly chill kind of guy in a beach city, but I do clothe myself with God spiritually.

Putting on the armor of God daily helps me go to battle as a warrior against the Darkness, human enemies, and the darkness of ego in humankind. Wearing the armor strengthens my soul to withstand any storm bending to no wind, lifting my shield to catch the flaming arrows of evil. I lift my bow and my arrow pointed towards God that carries his protection.

Know how much strength you have within you for access, even when you don't believe it's there. You know you have immense strength when you can endure a difficult circumstance and you still manage to move through it with finesse by running over that roadblock, resolving it, and then letting it go to move onto other things.

One of the top adjectives darted my way over the course of my life from others in-person is the word strong as well as independent. "God you're so strong. Wow you are really strong. You are way too strong. How are you so strong?"

I've always been a fighter by nature, which is part of the wise one warrior lineage among other things. It's part of the warrior nature to be primed for battle no matter what, and that stance can make one come off strong by comparison to someone else. Those around that know about my childhood abuse see that as a survivor, and so therefore must be strong. To me it's more than a survivor, but instead something I overcame. I gather repeated strength from Heaven every single day. There has never been a day that has gone by where I'm not in constant communication with God and my Spirit team. This strength is the fuel for the vehicle that drives me. My Spirit team's long running motto is to keep going. Gather strength from above and use that to persevere forward. God and your Spirit team are the sole ones you can always count on and rely on.

There are so many things they've engrained in me about persistence. Pull yourself up by your bootstraps and be the manager of your life controlling who and what is allowed in your vicinity. See the bigger picture above the physical life monotony and the drama. View life circumstances from the perspective of an angel. We were called to experience the Darkness to be able to efficiently guide others out of it and into the Light. We have a greater understanding of the human condition because we don't shy away from suffering through the differing levels of darkness that others find themselves trapped in. We have a larger understanding than others because we've touched every color of the palette that as human beings we can fall prey to. It's more than studying it, but it includes living it and immersing yourself into it. It's walking in someone else's shoes to gain empathic insight and perception.

God has not been easy on me. I don't always receive a bunch of miracle blessings and deliverances. I understood why God made me walk the path and believe me He made me walk that path covered with pain inducing nails and thorns. He wanted me to understand and relate to what people are going through by putting me through it too. This way I can give them hope in their battles that they'll make it. Sometimes God will make you go through something that doesn't make sense. It is expressly for the purpose of using you in that area to bring other people through to freedom at a later time in your life. Sometimes you do have to step out of the box on occasion in order to broaden your perception, see certain things in a different light, expand your consciousness, and have a better understanding of oneself.

Earth is not the souls natural home and much of someone's behavior is not your soul's natural behavior, except for when you are operating from the highest vibrational space a human being can reach. Each soul radiates a different degree of light depending on the wisdom it holds. Someone that has a great deal of knowledge radiates the brightest. The darker souls have a flicker of dim light. The greatest challenge is the opposing perceptions between soul and body. This is what all wrestle with this lifetime. The one that learns to master it is able to merge the two brilliantly. You know that what you accomplish this lifetime is meaningless unless it benefits others. Benefiting yourself is benefiting the ego and the flesh. Your talents and gifts are what are given to you by God for the positive benefit of others.

The highest vibrational energy that exists is love. This isn't to be confused with the kind of love bond two people have, but this is more of a universal love. To understand love is to be able to peer into the heart of a human being. The heart part of you is your soul. It is who you truly are behind the physical and personality part of yourself. This means judging anyone in anyway on appearances means you will have to take accountability for that one day. The physical limitations can make it challenging for someone to break through human superficiality and get into the soul of another person. Only an accelerated soul can get in there and be able to see who someone is. It's being able to see the true soul of the cruelest man. That's not a task that the ego has any interest in. When you judge on the surface, then you can't protest to know about love. Being unable to see the truth and soul of the most difficult person to love destroys your own spirit.

Love is the most powerful vibration that exists through time and space. One of the reasons that many don't show love is because to show love takes effort. Showing hatred is easy, but love...that's something else entirely. Love will always cost you something, whether that's time or energy. Love will cost you pride when you need to not let your ego dominate and let certain things go that someone else did.

Wisdom is having the knowledge about a subject, but

knowledge is about acquiring information, facts, or skills surrounding a subject. Gaining knowledge is easy, but gaining wisdom is difficult because it requires someone to take that knowledge and be able to practically apply it to their life effectively.

Many experience difficulties in the world. Maybe your situation is financial or you've lost your job and need a job. The good news is God knows it. He knew it before you ever entered into that struggle and He has your relief on His mind and His plan for you. You might be surprised by things that happen to you, but God is not surprised. He sees you, he knows you, he cares about you, and you will come through any struggle and challenge thrown at you. Never give up, because God loves you and He is bigger than your problems.

Ask God and your Spirit team daily to help you experience joy, to strengthen you, help you focus on what's important, and to fill you up with holy determination that you will never give up. Be thankful and grateful when every need is met. I've had to learn that the greater the mission God has for you, then the greater the demons you'll have to slaughter. When you rise into warrior mode, then you're strong enough to withstand any challenge and hardship, because you are a reed that bends to no wind. Stay centered psychic warrior and know that without a doubt in your consciousness that you are surrounded by high vibrational heavenly beings that want to help you reach your souls higher destination.

"Be a sober and vigilant spirit, be on the alert, because your adversary the devil prowls around like a lion roaring in fierce hunger seeking someone to devour." - Peter 5:8

Acknowledgments

Thank you to God, my Spirit Team Council, and to all of
the loyal readers that have hopped on this awesome train
ride of mine and stayed on. I am forever blessed and
grateful for your eternal support of the work we do.
Thank you also for supporting the arts and the artists of
the world.

Entertainment Films Mentioned in this Book

The Case for Christ
The Conjuring
Defending Your Life
Ghost
The Gift
Harry Potter
Hereafter
Indiana Jones
Limitless
Lord of the Rings
Lucy
The Never Ending Story
The Nightmare Before Christmas
Poltergeist
The Silence of the Lambs

Kevin Hunter

ALSO AVAILABLE BY KEVIN HUNTER

Books that Empower, Enlighten, Educate, and Entertain!

*Just as your body needs physical food to survive,
your soul needs spiritual food for well-being nourishment.*

A Beginner's Guide to the
FOUR PSYCHIC CLAIR SENSES

Many believe psychic gifts are bestowed upon select chosen ones, while others don't believe in the craft at all. The reality is every soul is born with heightened psychic gifts and capabilities, but somewhere along the way those senses have dimmed. All are capable of being a conduit with the other side, including those closed off and blocked to it. There are a variety of enlightened beings residing in the spirit realms to assist human souls that request their help. They use varying means and methods to communicate with you called clair channels. These clairs are crystal clear etheric senses used to communicate with any higher being, spirit guide, angel, departed loved one, archangel, and God.

The *Four Psychic Clair Senses* illustrates what the core senses are, examples of how the author picks up on messages, how you can recognize the guidance, and other fun metaphysical psychic stuff. You are a walking divination tool that allows you to communicate with Spirit. The clairs enable you to receive heavenly messages, guidance, and information that positively assist you or another along your Earthly journey. Read about the four core clairs in order to pinpoint what best describes you and how to have a better understanding of what they are and how they work for you.

TAROT CARD MEANINGS

Tarot Card Meanings is an encyclopedia reference guide that takes the Tarot apprentice reader through each of the 78 Tarot Cards offering the potential general meanings and interpretations that could be applied when conducting a reading. The meanings included can be applied to most anything whether it be spiritual, love, general, or work related questions.

Many novices struggle with reading the Tarot as they want to know what a card can mean in their readings. They grow stuck staring at three cards side by side and having no idea what it could be telling them. The Tarot Card Meanings book can assist by pointing you in the general direction of where to look. It will not give you the ultimate answers and should not be taken verbatim, as that is up to you as the reader to come to that conclusion. The more you practice, read, and study the Tarot, then the better you become.

Tarot Card Meanings avoids diving into the Tarot history, or card spreads and symbolism, but instead focuses solely on the potential meaning of a card in a general, love, or work reading. This gives you a structure to jump off of, but it is up to you to take that energy and add the additional layers to your reading, while trusting your higher self, intuition, instincts and Spirit team's guidance and messages. Anything included in the Tarot Card Meanings book is an overview and not intended to be gospel. It is merely one suggested version of the potential meanings of each of the 78 Tarot cards in a reading. It may assist the novice that is having trouble interpreting cards for themselves.

THE ESSENTIAL KEVIN HUNTER COLLECTION

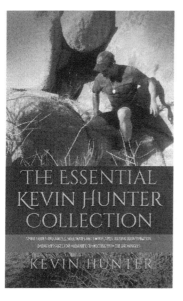

Kevin Hunter an empowering author specializing in a variety of genres, but he is most notably known for his work in the realms of spirituality, metaphysical, and self-help. He has assisted people around the world with standing in their power, and in having a stronger connection with Heaven, while navigating the materialistic practical world. Now some of his popular spiritually based books are available in this one gigantic volume.

The Essential Kevin Hunter Collection is the spiritual bible that contains over 500 pages of content geared towards improving and enhancing your life. It is for those who prefer to have everything in one gigantic book. The content included in this edition are from the books: *Spirit Guides and Angels, Soul Mates and Twin Flames, Raising Your Vibration, Divine Messages for Humanity, Connecting with the Archangels, Warrior of Light, Empowering Spirit Wisdom, and Darkness of Ego.*

THE ESSENTIAL
KEVIN HUNTER
COLLECTION

Featuring the following books
Warrior of Light, Empowering Spirit Wisdom, Darkness of Ego,
Spirit Guides and Angels, Soul Mates and Twin Flames, Raising
Your Vibration, Divine Messages for Humanity and Connecting
with the Archangels

TRANSCENDING UTOPIA
Reopening the Pathway to Divinity

Transcending Utopia is packed with practical and spirit knowledge that focuses on enhancing your life through empowering divinely guided spiritual related teachings, inspiration, wisdom, guidance, and messages. The way to accelerate existence on Earth towards Utopia is if every person on the planet resided in their soul's true nature, which is in a state of all love, joy, and peace. The ultimate Nirvana is surpassing that perfection through methods that a limited consciousness could ever dream possible. This is the exceptional glory your soul was born into

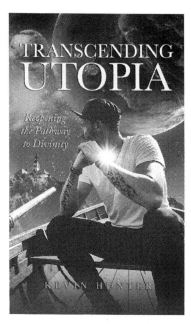

before the dense turbulence of Earthly life enveloped and suffocated you.

Transcending Utopia is to go beyond your limits and travel outside of the generic mundane materialistic achievement that human beings taught one another to thrive for. A utopian society is where everything is perfectly blissful on all levels according to the sanctified values you were born with. The sensations connected to how flawless everything feels in that moment reveals the authentic perfection you were made from. Utopia is the ideal paradise as imagined in one's dreams that seems to be inaccessible by human standards. It is a state of mind that is possible to reach by adopting broader ways of looking at circumstances while being disciplined about how you conduct your life. You search for a sign of this utopia through external means, only to be consistently left with disappointment. This is because utopia begins and ends inside the spark that burns within your spirit like a pilot light waiting to be ignited.

WARRIOR OF LIGHT
Messages from my Guides and Angels

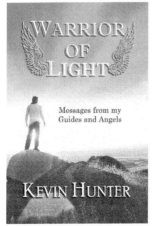

There are legions of angels, spirit guides, and departed loved ones in heaven that watch and guide you on your journey here on Earth. They are around to make your life easier and less stressful. Learn how you can recognize the guidance of your own Spirit team of guides and angels around you. Author, Kevin Hunter, relays heavenly guided messages about getting humanity, the world, and yourself into shape. He delivers the guidance passed onto him by his own Spirit team on how to fine tune your body, soul and raise your vibration. Doing this can help you gain hope and faith in your own life in order to start attracting in more abundance.

EMPOWERING SPIRIT WISDOM
A Warrior of Light's Guide on Love, Career and the Spirit World

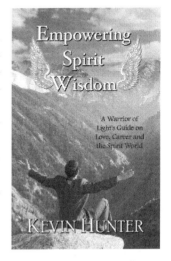

Kevin Hunter relays heavenly, guided messages for everyday life concerns with his book, *Empowering Spirit Wisdom.* Some of the topics covered are your soul, spirit and the power of the light, laws of attraction, finding meaningful work, transforming your professional and personal life, navigating through the various stages of dating and love relationships, as well as other practical affirmations and messages from the Archangels. Kevin Hunter passes on the sensible wisdom given to him by his own Spirit team in this inspirational book.

DARKNESS OF EGO

In *Darkness of Ego*, author Kevin Hunter infuses some of the guidance, messages, and wisdom he's received from his Spirit team surrounding all things ego related. The ego is one of the most damaging culprits in human life. Therefore, it is essential to understand the nature of the beast in order to navigate gracefully out of it when it spins out of control. Some of the topics covered in *Darkness of Ego* are humanity's destruction, mass hysteria,

karmic debt, and the power of the mind, heaven's gate, the ego's war on love and relationships, and much more.

REACHING FOR THE WARRIOR WITHIN

Reaching for the Warrior Within is the author's personal story recounting a volatile childhood. This led him to a path of addictions, anxiety and overindulgence in alcohol, drugs, cigarettes and destructive relationships. As a survival mechanism, he split into many different "selves". He credits turning his life around, not by therapy, but by simultaneously paying attention to the messages he has been receiving from his Spirit team in Heaven since birth.

235

REALM OF THE WISE ONE

In the Spirit Worlds and the dimensions that exist, reside numerous kingdoms that house a plethora of Spirits that inhabit various forms. One of these tribes is called the Wise Ones, a darker breed in the spirit realm who often chooses to incarnate into a human body one lifetime after another for important purposes.

The *Realm of the Wise One* takes you on a magical journey to the spirit world where the Wise Ones dwell. This is followed with in-depth and detailed information on how to recognize a human soul who has incarnated from the Wise One Realm.

Author, Kevin Hunter, is a Wise One who uses the knowledge passed onto him by his Spirit team of Guides and Angels to relay the wisdom surrounding all things Wise One. He discusses the traits, purposes, gifts, roles, and personalities among other things that make up someone who is a Wise One. Wise Ones have come in the guises of teachers, shaman, leaders, hunters, mediums, entertainers and others. *Realm of the Wise One* is an informational guide devoted to the tribe of the Wise Ones, both in human form and on the other side.

LIVING FOR THE WEEKEND
The Winding Road Towards Balancing Career Work and Spiritual Life

Working hard to ensure your bills are paid can leave your soul spiritually starved for soul nourishment. When your ultimate goal is to obtain enough money to be comfortable that you become carried away in that current, then there is little to no room for Divine enrichment.

Many work to survive in jobs they hate because it's the way it is. As a result, they experience and endure all sorts of emotional pain whether it is through depression, sadness, anger, or any other kind of negative stressor. Some silently suffer through this emotional strain gradually killing off their life force. If you don't have a healthy social life and positive fun filled activities and hobbies to balance that burden outside of that, then that could add additional tension. What's it all for if you can't live the life you've always wanted to live? Instead, you spend your days growing forever miserable and broken.

Living for the Weekend examines the pitfalls, struggles, as well as the benefits available in the current modern day working world. This is followed up with spiritual and practical tips, guidance, messages, and discussions on ways to incorporate more balance and enlightenment to a cutthroat material driven world.

Attracting in Abundance

Opening the Divine Gates to Inviting in Blessings and Prosperity Through Body, Mind, and Soul Spirit

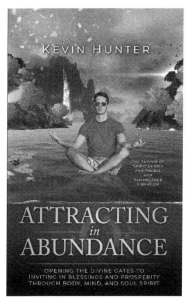

When you hear the word abundance, you may equate it to being blessed with a plentiful overflowing amount of money that equates to a big lottery win. Having enough money to survive comfortably enough on this physical plane is part of obtaining abundance, but it's not the destination and purpose to thrive for. You could work hard to make enough money to the point you are set for life, but that won't necessarily equate to happiness. Achieving a content satisfied state of joy and serenity starts with examining your soul's state and overall well-being. When that's in place, then the rest will follow.

Attracting in Abundance combines practical and spirit wisdom surrounding the nature of abundance. This is something that most everyone can get on board with because all human beings desire physical comforts, blessings, and prosperity, regardless of their personal values and belief systems. *Attracting in Abundance* is broken up into three parts to help move you towards inviting abundance into your life on all levels. "Part One" contains some no-nonsense lectures surrounding the philosophies, concepts, and debates on the laws of attracting in abundance. "Part Two" is the largest of the sections geared towards fine tuning the soul into preparing for abundance. "Part Three" is the final lesson plan to help crack open the gates of abundance with various helpful tidbits, guidance, and messages as well as the blocks that can prevent abundance from coming in.

The B-Side to the Attracting in Abundance book

ABUNDANCE ENLIGHTENMENT
*An Easy Motivational Guide to
the Laws of Attracting in Abundance
and Transforming Your Soul*

Ultimate authentic success surrounds your soul's growth and evolving process. It's when you realize that none of the physical ego driven desires matter in the end. You can work hard to make sure you stay afloat, you're able to pay your bills, and support yourself and family, but you're not chasing popularity for external validation. Any amount of goodness displayed from your heart is the true measure of real accomplishment.

An overflowing feeling of optimism and love coupled with faith and action is what increases the chances of attracting good things and positive experiences to you. Abundance is more than monetary and financial increase. It can also be about reaching an optimistic well-being state of joy, peace, and love. This positive emotional mindful state simultaneously attracts in blessings.

Abundance Enlightenment is the follow up book to *Attracting in Abundance*. It contains both practical guidance and spirit wisdom that can be applied to everyday life. Some of the key topics surround the laws of attraction as well as healthier money management and improving your soul to help make you a fine tuned in abundance attractor.

MONSTERS AND ANGELS

An Empath's Guide to Finding Peace in a Technologically Driven World Ripe with Toxic Monsters and Energy Draining Vampires

Every person on the planet is capable of being empathic and sensitive, to becoming an energy vampire or toxic monster. No one is exempt from displaying the darker sides of their ego. The easiest and most efficient way to spread any kind of energy is online. Every time you log onto the Internet, there is a larger chance you're going to see something related to the news, media, or gossip areas thrown in front of you, even if you attempt to avoid it as much as possible. You're absorbing everything that your consciousness faces, including the ugly and the wicked, which has its own consequences. This tempestuous energy is tossed into the Universe ultimately creating a flame-throwing battleground inside and around you.

Monsters and Angels discusses how technology, media, and social media have an immense power in distributing both positive and negative influences far and wide. This is about being mindful of what can negatively affect your state of being, and how to counter and avoid that when and wherever possible. This is why it's beneficial to govern yourself, your life, and your surroundings like a strict disciplined executive.

TWIN FLAME SOUL CONNECTIONS

*Recognizing the Split Apart, the Truths and Myths of Twin Flames,
Soul Love Connections, Soul Mates, and Karmic Relationships*

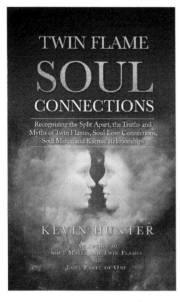

Twin Flames have a shared ongoing sentiment and quest from the moment they're a spark shooting out of God's love that explodes into a blinding white fire that breaks apart causing one to be two, until two become one again, separate and whole, and back around again. Looking into the eyes of your Twin Flame is like looking into the eyes of God, because to know love is to know God.

When one thinks of a Soul Mate or Twin Flame, they might equate it to a passionate romantic relationship where you're making love on a white sandy palm tree lined beach in paradise for the rest of your lives. This beautiful mythological notion has caused great turmoil in others who long for this person that fits the description of a lothario character in a romance novel. It is also an unrealistic and misguided interpretation of the Soul Mate or Twin Flame dynamic.

Twin Flame Soul Connections discusses and lists some of the various myths and truths surrounding the Twin Flames, and how to identify if you've come into contact with your Twin Flame, or if you know someone who has. The ultimate goal is not to find ones Twin Flame, but to awaken ones heart to love, and to work on becoming complete and whole as an individual soul through spiritual self-mastery, life lessons, growth, and raising your consciousness. Your soul's life was born out of love and will die right back into that love.

IGNITE YOUR INNER LIFE FORCE

Ignite Your Inner Life Force is an introduction guide for teens, young adults, and anyone seeking answers, messages, and guidance and surrounding spiritual empowerment. This is from understanding what Heaven, the soul, and spiritual beings are to knowing when you are connecting with your Spirit team of Guides and Angels. Some of the topics covered are communicating with Heaven, working with your Spirit team, what your higher self is, your life purpose and soul contract, what the ego is, love and relationships, your vibration energy, shifting your consciousness and thinking for yourself even when you stand alone. This is an in-depth primer manual offering you foundation as you find a higher purpose navigating through your personal journey in today's modern day practical world.

AWAKEN YOUR CREATIVE SPIRIT

Your creative spirit is more than being artistic and getting involved in creativity pursuits, although this is a good part of it. When your creative spirit is activated by a high vibration state of being, then this is the space you create from. You can apply this to your dealings in life, your creative and artistic pursuits, and to having a greater communication line with your Spirit team on the Other Side. *Awaken Your Creative Spirit* is an overview of what it means to have access to Divine assistance and how that plays a part in arousing the muse within you in order to bring your state of mind into a happier space.

THE *WARRIOR OF LIGHT* SERIES OF POCKET BOOKS

Spirit Guides and Angels, Soul Mates and Twin Flames, Raising Your Vibration, Connecting with the Archangels, Twin Flame Soul Connections, Attracting in Abundance, Monsters and Angels, The Four Psychic Clair Senses, The Seven Deadly Sins, Love Party of One, Abundance Enlightenment, and Divine Messages for Humanity

About the Author

Kevin Hunter is the metaphysical author of dozens of spiritually based books that include *Warrior of Light, Transcending Utopia, Stay Centered Psychic Warrior, Empowering Spirit Wisdom, Realm of the Wise One, Reaching for the Warrior Within, Darkness of Ego, Living for the Weekend, Ignite Your Inner Life Force, Awaken Your Creative Spirit,* and *Tarot Card Meanings.*

His pocket books include, *Spirit Guides and Angels, Soul Mates and Twin Flames, Raising Your Vibration, Divine Messages for Humanity, Connecting with the Archangels, The Seven Deadly Sins, Four Psychic Clair Senses, Monsters and Angels, Twin Flame Soul Connections, Attracting in Abundance, Love Party of One* and *Abundance Enlightenment.* His non-spiritual related works include the horror drama, *Paint the Silence,* and the modern day love story, *Jagger's Revolution.*

Kevin started out in the entertainment business in 1996 as the personal development assistant guy to one of Hollywood's most respected acting talents, Michelle Pfeiffer, at her former boutique production company, *Via Rosa Productions.* She dissolved her company after several years and he made a move into coordinating film productions for the studios. His film credits include *One Fine Day, A Thousand Acres, The Deep End of the Ocean, Crazy in Alabama, The Perfect Storm, Original Sin, Harry Potter & the Sorcerer's Stone, Dr. Dolittle 2,* and *Carolina.* He considers himself a beach bum born and raised in Southern California. For more information and books visit: www.kevin-hunter.com

Made in the USA
Las Vegas, NV
20 January 2024

84662134R00142